# THE DEBT RELIEF PLAYBOOK

(HOW TO DEFEAT CREDITORS AND
WIN THE COLLECTION WAR)

**A Legal Playbooks® Publication**

**LegalPlaybooks.com**

# The Debt Relief PLAYBOOK

## (HOW TO DEFEAT CREDITORS AND WIN THE COLLECTION WAR)

**MARK WESBROOKS, J.D.**
Board Certified, Creditors' Rights Law, American Board of Certification

A **Legal Playbooks®** Publication
**www.legalplaybooks.com**

**THE WESBROOKS INSTITUTE, L.L.C.**

LEGAL PLAYBOOKS® is a series of publications providing consumers to information, strategies, and techniques that may be utilized to achieve asset protection, debt relief and financial freedom. Special Editions have been published with respect to specific types of debts, and with respect to specific jurisdictions and territories throughout the United States and specific Nations of the world. More information about such publications is available at www.legalplaybooks.com

SIXTH EDITION

Library of Congress Cataloging-in-Publication Data has been applied for.

Cataloging information
ISBN 10: 1940125081
ISBN 13: 978-1940125084

Acknowledgments:

Cover Design: Derek Murphy, creativeindie.com

**LegalPlaybooks.com**

# *Contents*

# THE DEBT RELIEF PLAYBOOK

(HOW TO DEFEAT CREDITORS AND
WIN THE COLLECTION WAR)

**A Legal Playbooks® Publication**

**LegalPlaybooks.com**

# DEDICATION

For Chloe, Christian, Avanna and Cristalina.
My inspiration.

# *Preface*

Board Certified in Creditors Rights Law for 25 years by the American Board of Certification, Attorney Mark Wesbrooks details how little known provisions of law assure fairness and justice in Debtor/Creditor transactions, and how the American legal system provides tools and protections that can help to reduce and completely eliminate debt. America, with all of its ideals, has historically had a legal system that would cater to the powerful at the expense of the powerless. Over time, and through advancement of civil liberties and the hard work of consumer protection advocates, laws have been refined to enable citizens oppressed with debt to prevail against creditors and debt collectors who act improperly. Knowing how to use these laws has, in the past, required hiring a lawyer or getting an advanced legal education. That is no longer the case! Federal and State laws provide ammunition that levels the playing field for those who understand how to use these laws. This book reveals the steps and strategies to defeat creditors, debt collectors, and their attorneys in their efforts to collect upon invalid claims, as well as those who engage in illegal conduct in the process of collection. By understanding some basic principles and protections in the law, you can prevail against these creditors, debt collectors, and their attorneys, who intend to take your assets, invade your bank accounts, and garnish your paycheck. Preemptive action on your part (sending appropriate letters and documenting communications) may entirely eliminate the threat, without you ever having to defend a lawsuit or file for bankruptcy.

If a lawsuit is filed, you can defeat the case by raising proper defenses that apply to the collection case. Statistically, 35% of all debt lawsuits are completely meritless, yet result in default judgments against the consumer 93.4% of the time, as the result of the consumer's neglect to file a proper answer and raise basic defenses. Collectors and debt buyers prey on lower to middle class Americans, knowing that they cannot afford to hire a lawyer, and that they will not likely file any answer to oppose the lawsuit.

The Debt Relief Playbook is a step-by-step guide which provides the tools to level the playing field. If preemptive action is taken (i.e. sending properly-worded retaliatory letters that you have documented violations of federal and state laws such as the federal Fair Debt Collection Practices Act (FDCPA), Truth in Lending Act (TILA), Fair Credit Reporting Act (FCRA) and other state and federal laws, most debt collectors will close their files and their attorneys will recommend that the creditor not pursue the matter further.

This book enables you to understand and assert your legal rights and protections in times of battle, as opposed to surrendering in defeat. Creditors and collectors routinely commit violations of law in their efforts to collect and actually *owe you* money for their violations, as a matter of State and Federal law. When your family is under attack, it is time to fight. And when you fight, you must fight to win.

This book is one of a series of books published by Legal Playbooks® published to aid consumers in obtaining financial freedom, asset protection, and the good life guaranteed as part of the American Dream. Such dream still exists in America, but you must understand how to take control when confronted with aggressive creditors and collectors, whose sole mission is to financially gain by holding you to one-sided, oppressive (and often illegal) contracts.

Laws designed to protect consumers are only effective if you use them. Grasping the basic knowledge of these protections will assure that your dream will last for generations.

For information as to other valuable Legal Playbooks® publications, go to ***www.legalplaybooks.com***

# About the Author

Mark Wesbrooks is the founder of The Wesbrooks Institute. Wesbrooks has made a career of helping people free themselves from debt, having acted as a nationally board-certified attorney for thousands of clients in debt relief and bankruptcy matters over a period of 25 years. Wesbrooks has authored several publications, appeared as guest lecturer, and has litigated a number of landmark cases in federal and state Courts, including the Supreme Court of the United States. Wesbrooks maintains law offices in the States of Arizona and Texas. He has held national Board Certifications in the fields of Consumer Bankruptcy Law, Business Bankruptcy Law and Creditors' Rights Law through the American Board of Certification, having been one of only two Attorneys in the United States holding all three of such Certifications at such time. Wesbrooks now maintains a Board Certification nationally in the field of Creditors Rights Law, although his dedication and practice has been committed to representing individuals and small business owners.

Wesbrooks seeks preservation of justice and equal opportunity for all. He believes in holding accountable those who purposely seek to unfairly gain from others. Wesbrooks believes in the American dream.

# Introduction

This book is set out in three major parts. First, we will undertake to explore practices relating to getting and maintaining good debt, as a means of financing opportunities and necessities of life. Second, we will undertake a comprehensive review of laws that protect consumers from improper acts and practices of creditors, debt collectors and their attorneys. Finally, this book presents a step-by-step plan of attack, with sample letters, court pleadings, and strategies proven successful in defeating debt collectors and their attorneys in their attempts to collect their debts and added fees.

This Book provides examples of what conduct does or does not violate laws protecting consumers. These easy to read and follow examples will give the reader great insight on how to spot a violation of law, and how to place the creditor/collector on formal notice of a violation and lawsuit to come. These consumer protection laws, if violated, require that the debt collector compensate the consumer for damages in the event that even one single violation is proven. If you can establish even one violation, you will prevail on your claim against the creditor/collector. One violation can mean that the creditor/collector will be facing a class action case on behalf of all consumers affected by the violation, which means you have the tools to prevail against a threat of litigation. If an attorney is needed, the consumer can find a lawyer willing to work for free, based upon the expectation of the Court ordering the creditor/collector to pay his or her fees as the prevailing party.

This reality means that the consumer may now have an equal playing in battling the creditor/collector.

This Book contains a valuable Appendix ("The War Chest"), which contains the text of relevant consumer protection laws, sample letters to creditors, collectors and their attorneys, and sample court documents that may be filed in collection cases.

In addressing federal consumer protection laws available in United States, it is necessary to point out that there are eleven Circuit Courts in the United States, plus two additional Circuit Courts for the Federal and D.C. Circuits. Cases that have been decided by the Federal Circuit Courts provide different interpretations of the law. Where Circuit Courts make decisions that are in direct conflict, a litigant can petition to have the case decided by the United States Supreme Court. However, very few cases are ever accepted by the United States Supreme Court, which means that Circuit Court decisions will stand. The end result is that citizens of certain states may have different rights and protections than citizens living in other states. For example, most Circuit Courts allow removal and elimination of home-equity lines and second mortgages in Chapter 13 bankruptcy cases, where a minority of Circuit Courts do not permit such relief. This book will address the majority view in most States, with mention of the exceptions, where applicable. The good news is that no matter where you live, tremendous relief and protection is available to defeat creditors' attempts to invade your assets and income in effort to destroy your family.

# Chapter 1

## GOOD DEBT? IS THERE ANY SUCH THING?

"I'd rather go to bed without dinner than to rise in debt."
Benjamin Franklin

As true as the laws of nature, the laws of economics reveal that financial success is not generally achieved in America without either being born wealthy, or otherwise utilizing good debt. If you study the most successful people in American society, you will see that essentially all of them took their great financial leap to wealth through strategic use of good debt. Simple economics will tell you that if you can make a higher rate of return over a specified period of time than the cost of the debt to get there, you have made the right choice in using debt. However, any successful person will tell you that the world, like Mother Nature, is sometimes unpredictable, and that even good debt, if too much, can produce financial collapse and ruin. I remember in my younger days, when my father explained that if I wanted to get ahead in life, I needed to be ready and willing to take on risk. In discussing the idea of buying my first home, or undertaking a loan for a business idea, I would comment "but, what if...?," while my bold father would respond, "What if not?" Of course, those who succeed in becoming wealthy carefully evaluate risk and take care to avoid foreseeable losses. The choice of finding and securing good debt, as opposed to bad debt, is beyond the scope of this book, other than to say that debt with reasonable terms that allows you to access to the essentials of life (i.e. home, automobile, funds to start a business) is almost always good debt.

Lenders who provide this type of debt are very competitive, and the right terms for such debt can be found if you do your homework. As with other major choices in life, you must be leery of those who pump millions of dollars into mass advertising with promises to provide you so-called "easy" debt. You have to ask yourself, why would they spend so many millions of dollars to get my business, when this type of debt is readily available almost anywhere? Why do I see this commercial almost every time the late-night movie goes to break? Understand that lenders spend multi-millions of dollars to lure those who react impulsively, knowing that those who plan and research to fulfill their financial dreams will not likely fall prey to such advertising. Steer clear of the obvious and do your research. When you know that the benefits of a loan will far outweigh the cost, strike while the iron's hot. You don't want to be one of those who looks back up on your life and wonders "what might have been." By the same token, you don't want to be saying "what was I thinking?" Anyone who is intending to form a new business, build a real estate or asset-based company (sales, leasing, etc.) will need to utilize debt in order to finance their venture. Those in need of capital must be diligent in finding good debt, with fair terms, in order to ensure a successful outcome.

The ability to finance ideas and enterprises through good debt is absolutely essential to becoming wealthy in America. It is the core reason why you hear of the stories of people with humble backgrounds becoming the wealthiest members of society. Unless you were born wealthy, such "good debt" is essential to your achievement of wealth and the American dream. Those who understand the laws of nature understand that the seasons change, storm clouds bring rain, and to dress warm when it's cold. As is with the laws of nature, decisions and strategies that produce outcomes of success and wealth follow the same laws of cause and effect. Borrowing involves undertaking risk. You should study your credit options like a scientist, taking on only debt obligations that involve acceptable risks, in order to ensure good results.

## Getting and Maintaining Good Debt

The idea of giving and maintaining good debt may more correctly be stated as taking steps to avoid getting caught up in bad debt. Good debt is that necessary credit to obtain something (education, housing, business opportunity), with the idea that the purpose of the financing will increase your income earning potential.

## Educational Loans

Education is always a sound investment, as education provides the tools and credentials necessary to secure better employment and peer recognition. Furthermore, education gives you instant acceptance by those in need of the skills or services gained from your training. The simple fact that a person is a degreed professional places him or her in a position of high credibility and acceptance in the community, which translates into higher earning opportunities. After graduating from law school and becoming a lawyer, I often was confronted by high school and college students who would ask where was the best place to go to law school? Students are led to believe by elite society that it actually matters where they went to school. I assure you it does not. I have known several people who were accepted to attend a particular law school, which was low on the list of potential schools, but because the school was not the law school of their choice, they declined to attend law school. Their excuse was that they "tried," but did not get in where they wanted. My advice to anyone seeking a career in law is to attend any law school that will allow you the certification and privilege of the practice of law, as long as it is accredited to allow you the privilege to practice law in the State where you want to practice. A certificate from one law school has no greater value than another, if the individual holding those certificates may practice in the same profession, seek the same opportunities, and receive the same rewards. There are a vast variety of educational loans that are offered through federal and state programs. In financing my education, I did not learn until my second year of law school that there is a strategy in achieving grants, scholarships, and favorable student loans. You might think the strategies are complex. In fact, when dealing with grants (free money), I learned that the first individuals to turn in their student aid/loan applications (FAFSA), are the first to receive available grant money. After learning this, I literally showed up on the front steps of the financial aid office at 6:00 a.m. on the first date that such office began to receive and process financial aid applications. As I waited in a line of people for the doors of the financial aid office to open, I learned through conversations with others the strategy of assuring access to grant money and favorable student loans. I only wish I had learned the basic skill required to get access to this money three semesters sooner. Grants are resources that are very limited, such that they are processed on a first-come first-serve basis. Grant money available to students is usually gone within the first hours of processing applications, very much like concert tickets being sold out within the first hours of sale to those who camp out at the door of the ticket agency.

Educational loans are almost always good debt; however, students must learn to resist grabbing the easiest most accessible loans, and instead seek out and research the most favorable options.

**Exhaust All Alternatives to Incurring Student Loans**

First of all, you should always explore every opportunity to avoid incurring student loans. This includes saving money through a summer job and even selling things that you do not need. Keep reminding yourself that once you achieve your goal with education, gaining a steady income, that you will be able to buy these things again. Explore every opportunity for grants and government assistance that is out there. So many people believe that free money will only be provided for education if you get a scholarship. Yes, there are scholarship-based grants that are made available based on performance and achievement. However, there are also a great number of need-based grants. Get all of the information on these types of grants early in the game, as they are literally gone before most people even apply for them. Make friends with someone in the Financial Aid Office of the educational institution you are attending. More importantly, make sure that the person you do befriend is someone who actually works with and has direct personal knowledge of the details of processing applications for grants. While in law school, I formed a friendship within fifteen minutes in the Financial Aid Office of the University and was given the most valuable information which guaranteed me access to these valuable grants (now up to $6,195.00 per year for Pell Grants). In my situation, the simple advice was "get your financial aid application form fully prepared and filed early -- meaning on the first day (and in the first hours) that applications will be accepted." If your situation requires that you take out educational loans, you should study resources available in advance of entering into loans to finance your education. You want to be sure that you can have access to grants (free money) available, and that when you do take out a student loan, that you get the best terms available. There are many resources available that can assist you in gaining access to scholarships, grants, and student loans. Present tax law allows student loan interest to be tax deductible within defined limits.

Later in this book, we will review ways to reduce or eliminate student loans for those who are in trouble with such loans. Options to free yourself from student loan debt include the exercise of rights under federal law, which include regulations of the United States Department of Education and U.S. Bankruptcy laws. For a detailed plan of attack in reducing or eliminating student loans, read *The Student Loan Debt Relief Playbook,* also published as part of the Legal Playbooks series.

The fact that education equips you to earn more money, combined with the tax-deductible aspect of interest payments, means that student loans are usually "good" debt. By focusing on eliminating other bad debt, student loans can remain under control and within your monthly budget.

**Avoid Private Loans for Education.**

Once alternatives for scholarships, grants, and personal funds, are fully expended, you should then undertake to determine the best available student loan options. When considering student loans, you will be presented with government-backed loans, as well as offers from private lenders. Student loan lenders are often eager to make loans, for the reason that they know that such debts may not be eliminated in bankruptcy in the future. For this reason, it is critical that the terms of your loan are fair, and something that you will be able to pay back in the future, given the reasonable expectations of your income following graduation and gaining employment. I remember leaving the Financial Aid Office of the University where I was attending law school with a packet that set out hundreds of lenders names, addresses and telephone numbers. I was asked to "pick" which lender I wanted to use for my student loans. How bizarre such a question was for me as a student, who only cared for getting the loans approved. Such packet of information offered little assistance in understanding the terms for payback of these loans, and what options were available to me in the future if I was unemployed or had other financial difficulty. I always recommend utilizing resources available to assist in selecting the right loans, as such information is available through the United States Department of Education and other sources.

Recently, the federal government enacted legislation to remove the private lenders from the marketplace for student loans. The downside with that decision is that such government loans for education will likely remain non-dischargeable in bankruptcy proceedings, unlike other debts.

Again, the scope of this book is to enable the reader to be equipped to defeat creditors' efforts to collect through forced reduction or elimination of debt. Since student loans can often be the most difficult to eliminate, you must exercise extraordinary care in choosing the right loans, to assure terms that are fair and that you will have available remedies in the event of future financial hardship. These remedies are often a condition to the lender for the Federal Government to guarantee the loan. If the lender does not agree to these available remedies and conditions, the Federal Government will not guarantee payment of the loan. Private student loans, which are not guaranteed by the Federal Government or otherwise regulated to Federal or State agencies, do not offer these protections. And yet, simply because you used a federal application (FAF - Financial Aid Form FAFSA Application) in applying for financial aid, such private student loan may not be eliminated through Bankruptcy to the same extent as if it had been a government guaranteed loan, even though the loan has different terms, differing rights of deferment, or absence of other available remedies.

For detailed information and an attack plan for dealing with student loan lenders and their collectors, I recommend reading *The Student Loan Debt Relief Playbook.* Such book details remedies available against student loan creditors, including rights of deferments and loan forgiveness options. Rights and remedies are available under federal law, through the United States Department of Education (deferment, forbearance and forgiveness) as well as through the Bankruptcy Courts, which allow for reduction or elimination of student loans in situations of undue hardship. Such publication also provides information on defending a student loan litigation which 90% of the time is brought by one of the Student Loan Trusts who took the loans by assignment.

Laws and protective regulations are available to assure that you may avoid judgments and wage garnishments from student loan creditors, if you properly invoke the legal protections. If student loans are a big part of the problem, ***The Student Loan Debt Relief Playbook*** is an essential reading.

## Mortgages and Real Estate Financing

Real estate loans incurred for purposes of acquiring ownership of property are almost always considered to be good debt. Of course, that is assuming that the buyer of real estate understands the three golden rules of real estate acquisition: "Location, Location, Location!" Furthermore, you must understand when it is the time to buy and when it is the time to sell, just like with other investments. When the investment is a home that will provide shelter and a residence for you, a mortgage payment is a preferred option as opposed to a rental payment. In other words, you are paying for the price of housing, whether you own a home or not.

So how can a home mortgage ever be considered to be bad debt? At the time of writing this publication, as a bankruptcy attorney, I am assisting thousands of people in restructuring their mortgages, eliminating debts, and reorganizing through bankruptcy. I find many people who are abandoning their homes, are doing so for the reason that the market values as may be determined through online services such as *www.zilllow.com* reflect that the home was worth considerably less than the homeowner's mortgages. Many people tell me that they are leaving their home because, "I could pay on this mortgage for 10 more years, and I still won't have any equity!" I often find myself asking the question, "Can you find a place to live where you are as happy for a monthly rental payment that is less than your house payment?" Without trying to overly influence my client, I am trying to impress the reality that changes in the economy, although disappointing, do not change the fact that you need a place to live. Economic conditions inevitably improve, such that real estate has always proven to be a good investment. Never in the history of the world has real estate value continued in a downward direction, where population numbers are rising.

In the large population centers, economic change was dramatic with reported home values soaring far above realistic values of homes. It seemed that everyone in these metropolitan areas who owned a home were eager to buy that second home as an investment, if they had the ability to borrow the funds. Of course, lenders would make a loan to practically anyone, for the same reason -- it seemed impossible that money could not be fully recovered from the property, in the event of a default and foreclosure. When the market crashed, homeowners found themselves in a situation where they could not sell the home, even if the buyer came along who was willing to pay their price - the prospective buyer would have to go to the bank to get a loan to purchase the property. Lenders were not going for that, as property values were so far below what was required to purchase the home. Homeowners have now found themselves in situations where the buyers can't buy, and the sellers can't sell. Accordingly, the real estate investor is stuck with the home, which was purchased only out of the expectation that the buyer would hold and sell the property when the value of the property continued to rise. Buying property at market value, with an expectation to sell the property in the near future at a higher value (as if investing in a soaring stock) is never a wise investment. The situation is quite different if you can purchase the property far below market value, as is the case today with massive numbers of foreclosures.

If real estate is used as a residence or for a business, you cannot fail, as the reality is that in order to live or operate your business, you would otherwise have to pay rent to someone else. Incurring a mortgage payment for a home or a business location puts you in a rent-free situation, such that these type of mortgages are almost always good debt. Furthermore, ownership of real property and timely payment of mortgage payments build credit, produce a strong financial statement, and ultimately will allow building of equity in the property. Mortgage interest is tax deductible, which means more money in your pocket, and tax-free recovery of your equity when you sell. You cannot deduct rent for personal housing on your tax return. If you do some simple math, you will see that income taxes you pay are far less when you can deduct mortgage interest and property taxes paid from your gross annual income. In short, although a mortgage payment is debt, paying that mortgage reduces your taxes and builds equity in the property.

Finally, under income tax guidelines, if you sell your principal residence, profit you make on the sale (within defined limits) is tax free. Given expected economic conditions, even with the ups and downs, most homeowners come out ahead, and with all the tax benefits. After selling, homeowners are able to acquire a larger and more expensive home, simply because they made smart decisions in purchasing their last home. There are extraordinary incentives and programs available, to provide money to you in purchasing a home. There are government incentives and free money available for first time home buyers. Some local governments give away money or provide tax breaks for buyers who maintain special types (historical) properties or who buy in certain neighborhoods.

Under certain situations, Federal law allows reduction or complete eliminate of certain mortgage loans. In specific areas of the United States, second mortgages and home equity lines may be completely eliminated through specific legal proceedings. Foreclosures may be stopped, mortgages restructured, and arrearage paid over a period of up to five years at zero interest. This is a guaranteed right under federal law. These laws (Title 11, United States Code) and strategies are covered later in later Chapters of this book.

## Debt to Start or Operate a Business

Debt incurred for purposes of starting or operating a business is almost always good debt. Like any other forms of financing, you should shop around and pay careful attention to the terms of repayment and remedies of default. Many lenders who provide commercial loans will operate under circumstances where the loans are guaranteed by the United States Small Business

Administration (SBA). Such agency exists for purposes of providing guarantees to lenders that their loans would be repaid, if they will make loans to qualifying businesses and individuals for purposes of development of business enterprises. As with student loans, lenders are very competitive and offer favorable terms in order to make these loans, as they come almost risk-free when the government is guaranteeing repayment. Accordingly, terms of the small business loan guaranteed by SBA should be extraordinarily favorable with competitive market interest rates, or you should keep shopping for a better loan. Additionally, many state and local governments provide incentives for startup of small businesses that impact under-developed areas of society, contribute to the local economy, or otherwise promote the advancement of causes that promote citizenship. Grant and bond programs are available where communities have set money aside for purposes of promoting private businesses, thereby advancing the goals and policies of equality and citizenship. As with student loans, undertaking a small amount of research will lead you to free money for starting a new business.

## Automobile Loans
## Beat Them at Their Own Game!

Automobile loans are almost always bad debt. However, unlike credit card debt, a car loan is usually a nondiscretionary item. In order to live in our modern society, one must have a vehicle to get around. And besides, part of the American dream is to own your own car. The trick is to always be the winner when it comes to financing the purchase of your car. There are many traps for the unwary. If you understand the basic principles of financing and some of the tricks involved in sale and financing of cars, you will come out ahead.

Loans made through automobile dealerships account for 90% of all automobile loans. Primarily, such transactions arise out of convenience, for the reason that at the time the purchase decision is made for the car, the buyer is extraordinarily eager to drive off the lot with the new vehicle. This is a moment when the buyer feels excited and elated, since the time has finally arrived to drive off with his or her dream car. Unfortunately, automobile dealerships, through their finance offices, take extraordinary advantage of the car buyer to line their pockets. In fact, insiders in the world of car financing will attest that most dealerships make more money on the financing than on the actual sale of the vehicle. The first line of defense to these techniques is to prearrange financing through a bank or credit union, in advance of making your decision to purchase a car. Avoid entering into the conversation of "What payment can you afford?" which is always the first question that a car salesman asks you, when you ask, "What is the price of this car?" Why is that? Simply put, car salesmen and their managers clearly understand that if they can get that number from you, they can make that number work in a way to maximize their profits. For example, if a person says they can afford a payment of $450 per month, car salesmen and their finance office will plug that number into a loan that has the longest duration (now up to 7 years!!!), with the highest interest rate, and then lead you to the car that will provide the most profit to the dealer at the end of the day. It is for this reason that, when searching for a car, you should inform car salesman that you only wish to discuss cash price. If you do your homework prior to visiting the dealership, you will know approximately what price of the car that $450.00 per month will buy, under fair financing terms. Traditional lenders (Banks and Credit Unions) will pre-approve you for a cash purchase amount. Finally, after the car selected, you must understand that the sale is not over.

It is a fact that the "finance guy" is the highest paid employee in the dealership, as his salary is commissioned-based, depending on the interest rate that you agree when signing the purchase and financing contracts. Most of you who have been through the painful process of buying a car have likely noticed that the finance guy always gets up and leaves the room, thereafter returning with a proposal. If the proposal is unacceptable, after a long sales presentation, the finance guy will then get up and leave the room again, as if he going to do some hard work for you in some unknown secret room where the public is not invited. Usually, if the sale of financing is not going well, and the finance guy perceives that you're a hard negotiator, he will leave the room for an extraordinarily long period of time. This is done so that you believe he's working extraordinarily hard, on the phone with various lenders, and undertaking exhaustive efforts to find the best deal for you. In fact, what he is really drinking coffee down the hall with another employee. Finally, he returns with what appears to be a mass of paperwork (totally unrelated to your transaction), and pen behind his ear, again to give you an impression that he's been working hard to get you the best deal out there. He then characterizes the proposal as a "special limited offer," that will not be available for long, mentions incentives and pricing benefits that you already gained through the salesperson in getting the car of your dreams, and then, he will explain that there are problems with respect to your credit report, credit history, and overall other debt. Don't be surprised if you hear references to your monthly house payment, overall debt, or suggested problems with the banks in lenders that make loans hard to get. This is simply not true. In fact, I will give you proof! The next time you purchase a car, and for all such endeavors in the future, remember this strategy and you will defeat the predatory car lender. When you are finally in the finance office, after sealing the deal on your choice of vehicle, when you believe that your deal is finally made with the best option available, inform the person putting together your financing that, "When I leave your dealership, I am going to contact the lender that approved my loan. No offense to you and your dealership, but... if I learn that the Lender qualified me at a lower rate than you signed me, I am going to sue your dealership, and I have an attorney ready to go." What you will see will amaze you! You will see the person instantly offer to "run check for a moment" to be sure that this is the very best financing available. Again, he will leave the room for an extraordinarily long period of time, and you will feel like you are in the doctor's office waiting for lab results. When he finally comes back in the room, he will have a lower percentage rate to present to you. He is now offering a new proposal, solely to avoid getting caught in a lie, as he knows that the deal offered last round was a sham. In my legal career, I had the occasion to file a class-action lawsuit against a dealership for these practices. Plain and simply put, it is dishonest and fraudulent for a person to give the appearance that they are working for you to get you the best possible financing, when in fact, that person not working for you, and is making false representations to make more profit. Most financing is totally prearranged, and it doesn't take the degree of time and effort that you are led to believe in order to make a loan. The idea is that you will get so frustrated that you will finally grab the pen and say, "You know what? Let's just get this done."

These are skills and tricks of the finance employees in the dealership that are tried-and-true, having produced high profits and commissions for those sitting across the table from you. They know you are dying to get behind the wheel of your new car, which has been washed and is parked at the front of the dealership waiting for you for your pleasure, once you hurry up and sign necessary paperwork that gives you the keys.

With some consumer attorneys beginning to take action against these practices, dealers have sought additional ways to avoid being sued for their fraudulent practices. Now, if you turn over to the reverse side of the paperwork that you will be signing (which is usually on yellow or pink paper, with a light gray type -- designed to prevent you from being able to read it under fluorescent lights of the dealership), you will see that the automobile dealership will say something along the lines of: "Buyer is aware and consents to dealer receiving commission on financing."

So how do you overcome these tricks and practices that are so unfairly designed to reap profits from you? Simply inform the finance guy, before you sign that you intend to write below your signature **"DO NOT AGREE TO COMMISSION ON DEALER FINANCING."** Simply put, you are informing the finance person that you know the game that takes place in the dealership finance office, and that you are not open to the idea of an additional sale. You must firmly state that you will not close the deal on the vehicle without suitable financing. You did not come to the dealership for financing services, as you can get those from a bank or credit union.

Finally, it always helps to let them know that you have already undertaken the same efforts and procedures with another dealership, and that if you don't feel like you're being treated fairly, you will go with the other transaction. (Also, if you are buying a used car, let them know that you found a similar car that is for sale by a private owner, and that you can get the credit union to do the loan.) It does not serve you to provide any details as to the other prospective deal. If asked, simply state that that is irrelevant to the transaction at issue.

In my personal experience in financing vehicles, I had the finance person return to the office four separate times, each time with a lower interest rate. Of course, he tried to play all of the usual games with me, such as mentioning an extraordinarily favorable interest rate if the buyer advances a very large amount towards down payment. I called his bluff on this, and learned that there really was no such thing, he was just trying to suggest that the more favorable interest rate was available only to people who were willing to put up a large amount of money. He knows that the great majority of people are not prepared to make a large deposit of cash toward then transaction, so that the conversation will turn back to the high interest proposal he wants you to take. Interest rates are based upon risk and credit score, and generally not affected by the level of down payment. These type of unrealistic proposals are thrown at you simply to steer you into believing that the deal being proposed is actually a good deal given your specific financial circumstances.

It is almost always a certainty that you will not obtain as favorable of a deal on financing if you do so through the dealership. You must remember that the dealership is acting as a broker, meaning that they are a middleman between the lender and the borrower, who expects to receive a commission for putting together the loan. They know that their commissions will be great, and that tremendous profit may be achieved, for the reason that everyone sitting down at the table to enter into financing has the vehicle of their dreams ready to go with the keys in the ignition in the parking lot. This tremendous lure enables them to reap great profits. The sad reality is that the majority of people purchasing the car believe that the very first proposal is the best they could ever achieve. In fact, the salesperson has already made his way back to the finance office to reveal inside information about what you can afford to pay, so that they can put together a loan that reaps them the most profit. Did you ever wonder why the salesperson offers you cookies and lemonade, while he goes to the back of the dealership once or twice, while you are taking the final look over your vehicle? Also, wouldn't you think that the dealership would want to tell you the price of the vehicle in response to your first question, as opposed to hitting you up with the question about what you can afford? Anytime you ask a question, and it is answered with another question, you should be very suspect in the motive of that salesperson. This has always been the most aggravating part of my experience on a car lot. I would always say, I won't be financing, I will be paying cash. On such occasions, I clearly knew that I would never pay cash, and that I would be financing. However, this was my way of avoiding the gamesmanship on the part of car salesman, all designed to reap exorbitant profits from my need for transportation. Once the price of the car is agreed, then and only then is the time to discuss financing. The end result is more car for your money, with a lower monthly payment.

Banks, credit unions and other lenders not affiliated with car dealerships know that you are not 30 seconds away from jumping in your new car for your first pleasure drive home. Rather, such lenders know that you can leave the bank and do your further research at home. Accordingly, such lenders will attempt to demonstrate how their loan is or is not affordable to you, and if for some reason there is a credit issue, you walk away educated as to where the credit problem lies. Although you still have to be careful with banking lenders, the person assisting you with the loan is generally not a commission-based employee planning to receive a higher commission if you sign-on for a higher rate of interest loan. You will not see these lenders getting up, leaving the room for endless periods of time, and thereafter returning trying to convince you that they are working hard to get a better deal. Finally, this person is likely to get points, as opposed to commissions, which help them advance in their pay scale or rank at the bank, by closing the loan and presenting other services, like home equity loans, overdraft protection on accounts, and other services offered by the bank. I personally do not take offense at these lending officers trying to offer other products and promotions, as they are not trying to drive up the price of my car to line their pockets by presenting these additional products. You will find that you can meet with a lending officer at a bank or credit union to prearrange a car loan, allowing you to walk out the front door knowing what cash price of the car will fit in with the approved financing. Then, when you visit the automobile dealership, or when you search for a vehicle in the private market, you will only have to talk cash price of the car. By following these procedures, you have already saved thousands of dollars in interest charges that you otherwise will incur if you finance at the dealership. I learned very early in my career that your banker can prove to be a good friend. Always meet the branch manager, and even if you are at the bank on a minor issue, stop by and say "Hello." or at least give a wave to the branch manager on your way out of the bank. This person will bend over backwards for you when you later need something done. Name recognition, and the simple fact that you go out of your way to say "Hello" to this person each time you come to the bank, can open many doors for you, when you need to incur important loans in the future. If the Manager sees you waive on your way out of the Bank, and she doesn't know who you are, out of concern she will run over to the clerk you were dealing with and say, "Who was that?" The next time you go into the bank, the branch manager will waive to you and know your name.

Another sure way to save money is to find your vehicle in an automobile classified publication and purchase the vehicle from a private party. While you must be careful, and often will need to undergo an inspection of the vehicle prior to making your deal, you will find motivated sellers, and avoid incidental costs, taxes and other charges that you must pay when buying a car through dealership. The downside to a private party sale is that there is no warranty, and often no recourse against the seller, if you learn the vehicle has problems or was in a prior accident. So do your homework if you are going with a private sale transaction.

# CREDIT CARDS

By far, credit card debt is the worst type of debt to incur. It is generally the highest market rate of interest that you will pay for borrowing money. Additionally, credit card companies make millions, if not billions of dollars, from late fees, over limit fees, and other collateral charges associated with consumer credit card accounts. Consumers find it extraordinarily difficult, if not impossible, to climb out of deep credit card debt. Irrespective of this, it must be acknowledged that credit card debt is one of the easiest ways for consumers to access credit. Wise consumers will maintain their credit cards as an electronic checkbook with the credit card issuer providing itemization of charges, simplifying their lives in not having to carry around cash or a check book, and as a means to consolidate recordkeeping. Responsible users of credit cards maintain balances that do not exceed an amount which may be paid off in full before the next billing cycle. Others stay ahead of the game in maintaining credit cards with favorable rates (quite often 0%) and then accomplish a balance transfer before the favorable interest ends, and an excessive burdensome rate begins to be applied to the outstanding balance.

In retaliation towards prudent consumers, the credit card industry has developed methods to trap consumers into paying their high interest rates. For example, credit card issuers that offered favorable interest terms for transfer of a balance over to their cards, would apply excessively high interest rates to purchases made with the card, with the high interest debt from purchases becoming trapped below the favorable interest debt transferred to the card, Thereafter they apply payments received to the low interest debt first, never reducing the balance on the high interest debt until the low interest debt is paid off in full. Most consumers were not even aware of this until it was too late. Others simply have not had the time and energy to understand how this practice trapped them into high interest debt, until the debt spiraled out of control. New legislation passed by Congress is designed to protect consumers from some of these unfair tactics.

If you study the history of the credit card industry, you will learn that the credit card business is much like the casino gambling business. Just as with casinos, the credit card system is set up so that the house always wins. With casino gambling, the casino always knows that there will be jackpots throughout its casino, and that there must be payouts and dividends available to those who enter the casino doors, or otherwise to gamblers will not come. The lure and often irresistible temptation of having access to gambling winnings is enough to bring a huge mass of people and their money flowing through the casino. Mathematics, assure, with absolute certainty, that the casino always comes out ahead with big profits. The casino's games of chance all assure that, with a degree of mathematical certainty, the casino will always win and reap deep profits. Understanding that gambling, if continued, eventually drains the gambler's finances to the benefit of the casino, most state legislatures and governmental bodies prohibit such gambling operations in their states.

As with casinos, over a course of decades, the credit card industry has found itself confronted with state legislatures that have taken protective action on behalf of its consumers. Many may recall that years ago, when you received a credit card statement, in order to ascertain your interest rate, you had to look at the back of the statement, whereupon you would see something along the lines of "If you live in TX, FL, GA... your interest rate is 18.9%. If you live in AZ, CA, NV... your interest rate is 21.9%." The reason for this type of explanation of interest rate relative to the particular state where the consumer resided, was that each state legislature would decide the maximum interest rate that credit lenders could charge to their citizens.

Over the course of years, the credit card industry has prevailed in lobbying and influencing politicians to reap extraordinary financial gains. Just as gambling operations located themselves in the State of Nevada, credit card issuers began to locate themselves within states that would allow the charging of excessive interest rates. Laws were changed, such that the states no longer provided the consumer protection for its citizens. Legislatures would now regulate the credit card industry based upon, not where consumers lived, but where the credit card issuer was located. This was another political move designed to lure of a business into states remote from the population centers of America. For example, most of you know that when you make a credit card payment, you are usually sending it to the states of South Dakota, Nevada, or Arizona. The reason for this is that many years ago, the Governors of these states, along with a number of state politicians, decided that if they allowed credit card issuers located in their states to charge excessive interest rates, that the credit card issuers would migrate into their states, creating thousands of new jobs. As a political move to win votes and the favor of their citizens, state lawmakers betrayed consumers throughout the United States, throwing basic consumer protection out the window in order to raise tax revenues and provide more jobs at home.

# PROTECT YOURSELF! DEFENDING AGAINST CREDITORS

*"The only real defense is an active defense."* Mao Zedong

Given the fact that creditors unilaterally determine the environment of interest rates and terms of debt borrowing, it is essential that consumers arm and be prepared to defend themselves in situations where it is impossible to meet the creditor's demands. While laws are available to reduce or eliminate debts through bankruptcy, such measures may cause some people to lose assets and credit standing. By adequately arming yourself with knowledge and good strategies, a creditor's unfair and often illegal tactics may be defeated. In many cases, the debt collector's attack may be entirely defeated even before legal proceedings are filed in Court. Defeating unethical debt collectors and their attorneys will help you provide for your family's protection and wellbeing, without disruption and losses which can have an impact for generations. Follow the road map that I will give you, and you will prevail!

# Chapter 2

# RULES OF ENGAGEMENT

> For we wrestle not against flesh and blood, but against principalities, against powers, against the rulers of the darkness of this world, against spiritual wickedness in high places. *Holy Bible, The Book of Ephesians*, Chapter 6, verse 12.]

Defeating creditors and their collectors who violate the law is highly probable if you understand your legal rights and recognize their violations of law. Properly asserting those rights and protections will allow you to prevail, defeating their unlawful efforts. These claims may be raised at all stages of the Creditor's collection efforts, and may be asserted as counter-claims if the Creditor files a lawsuit. However, if you do not timely and properly assert your rights, your rights may later be deemed waived by the Courts.

## Fair Debt Collection Practices Act (FDCPA)

The Fair Debt Collections Practices Act (also called the FDCPA) requires that debt collectors conform to strict rules and requirements in attempting to collect debts. Federal law allows you to recover from the creditor the sum of $1,000.00 as statutory damages plus any and all actual damages or losses suffered. The collector who violates the FDCPA must also pay all of your attorney fees, should you have to use an attorney. A debt collector who violates the FDCPA may owe you far more than the amount of the debt that they are trying to collect, as many collectors who break the law will commit multiple violations, which can add up to many thousands of dollars that they have to pay you and your lawyer. State laws may also require that the collector pay additional damages for debt collection violations.

## Fair Credit Reporting Act (FCRA)

The Fair Credit Reporting Act (also called the FCRA) deals with credit reporting issues. Adverse credit reporting to credit bureaus can affect your ability to have access to credit, which can prevent you from function normally in society. Violations of the FCRA can give rise to additional penalties to the creditor or reporting entity. Posting inaccurate information to credit bureaus, available to future creditors to see, can inflict serious harm. Creditors who violate the FCRA may be held liable to the consumer for actual damages incurred, which may include recovery of emotional distress and embarrassment. If the false reporting of your credit was willful, the Court can order payment of punitive damages (additional monetary damages to punish the offending party). Actual damages may include damages related to the additional cost of credit because of the false report (i.e. higher interest charges), emotional distress, embarrassment, and may even include payment of your attorney's fees incurred in correcting the false report. Under the FCRA, even if the creditor or reporting entity did not purposely make the false report, they may be held liable for negligent reporting. (Negligence requires a showing of failure on the part of the creditor/reporting entity to have exercised a reasonable degree of care in determining accuracy.) Some States have additional provisions in their law that may increase the amount of money to be paid to the consumer for violations of the FCRA and the State's law protecting consumers.

## The Truth in Lending Act (TILA)

The Truth in Lending Act (TILA) requires truthfulness on the part of the creditor in its contracts, credit applications, and other documentation utilized as part of a lending transaction. Violation of provisions of the TILA gives the consumer the right to collect statutory damages (i.e. collecting double the amount of finance charges assessed against the consumer), as well as other actual damages or losses incurred. A creditor who violates the TILA will also have to pay all of your costs and attorney fees. Since TILA cases usually involve problems with the creditor's paperwork, even one violation will enable an attorney to request that the case proceed as a Class Action lawsuit on behalf of all consumers who received the same paperwork. A creditor who violates the TILA will act quickly to settle your complaint, understanding that your case could be presented as a class action suit on behalf of everyone affected. Class actions are very expensive for creditors, and an offending creditor will undergo extreme efforts to avoid them. Many States have additional consumer protection laws which punish Creditors who violate Truth in Lending laws.

The Truth in Lending Act also governs advertisements and promotional literature that make credit offers. Creditors may not be deceptive in their advertising, and thereafter bind consumers to contracts that have less favorable terms than the advertisements that attracted the consumer.

The Truth in Lending Act also applies to home-equity lines of credit. If the lender violates TILA, a homeowner may completely rescind (void) the home-equity line agreement, forcing the home-equity lender to entirely lose its lien on the home, preventing any subsequent foreclosure.

## The Credit Card Accountability Responsibility and Disclosure Act (The CARD Act)

As of 2019, there are over 336 million active credit cards in the United States. That's more than one credit card for every living person in the U.S. (even children). In 2009, Congress passed the CARD Act, which requires financial institutions to disclose vital information when issuing new credit cards. This legislation, and through recent amendments, provided rules to credit card companies for purpose of protecting consumers from big surprises an undisclosed fees and costs. The CARD Act includes the following protections:

- Card companies may only increase credit limit after considering the consumers ability to pay.
- Credit card issuers have to give 45-days notice before charging a higher interest rate.
- A minimum 21-day grace period must be allowed before a due date for a payment.
- Fees for mail, phone or electronic payments are eliminated.

- Fees cannot be charged for over limit transactions unless the consumer "opts in" to this form of protection.
- Gift items can no longer be offered as incentives for signing up for cards.

## State Law Consumer Protection Statutes

In addition to federal law remedies, each state in the United States has its own set of laws that govern the dealings between debtors and creditors. In most instances, state laws work together with Federal Law, so that you can present claims for violations of both federal and state law. Many states have laws that give consumers remedies for deceptive trade practices occurring in the process of incurring debt, or with respect to the sale transaction that created the debt obligation. It is important to be aware of applicable state laws, as there may be additional remedies that the federal law does not provide (i.e. tripling of the amount of damages suffered by the consumer, or allowing additional recovery additional damages not available under the federal law).

Each state has its own set of rules with respect to what steps a creditor must undertake to secure a court judgment. If a creditor takes a judgment against the debtor, it is the state law that will determine what property can be reached, and what property is protected. Some states have very strong protection to its citizens (i.e. Texas and Florida have unlimited homestead protections – meaning the home is protected irrespective of value, even if it's worth millions of dollars; some states prohibit garnishment of wages – North Carolina, South Carolina, Texas). Other states offer very little protection for its citizens (i.e. Pennsylvania has no homestead protection, no vehicle protection, and allows only $300.00 worth of property to be protected from creditors). Most other States permit wage garnishments to pay creditors.

## Other Federal Laws Protecting Consumers

Title 11 of the United States Code (commonly known as the "Bankruptcy Code") provides protection to consumers in debt, irrespective of the State where a consumer happens to reside. Federal bankruptcy law permits an individual to receive a legal discharge (legal forgiveness) of their debts. Debts that are discharged in bankruptcy are permanently removed, and may not be revived over the debtor's lifetime or against the debtor's estate upon death. Bankruptcy discharge provides the ultimate protection from creditors, as federal bankruptcy laws completely supersede state law, providing relief from creditors. Relief that may be afforded under the federal bankruptcy laws depends on the income and assets of the debtor who files bankruptcy. The bankruptcy laws ensure that a person may not be impaired by their creditors to a point where he or she cannot provide for the family. Bankruptcy law allows the lowering of payments on debts that a consumer needs to pay off (automobiles, mortgages and others), while providing a discharge as to those debts that a debtor cannot afford to pay (credit card, medical bills, and other unsecured debts).

# Chapter 3

# LEVELING THE PLAYING FIELD

"This is not a contest between persons. The humblest citizen in all the land, when clad in the armor of a righteous cause, is stronger than all the hosts of error." *William Jennings Bryan*

When the playing field is level, such that the debtor and creditor are equipped with the same level of knowledge and understanding of legal rights and responsibilities, the outcome of a debtor/creditor dispute is more likely to be a fair and just result. The purpose of this book is not to teach how to defeat legitimate obligations, but rather, to hold creditors and debt collectors accountable for their violations of the law. To the extent they choose to violate their responsibilities, or otherwise if they fail to exercise reasonable care (are negligent) with respect to the processing of their claim, they will have to pay damages caused to the consumer. Damages suffered by the consumer often exceed the dollar amount of the original debt. Experience has shown me that in situations where each side of a dispute has a legitimate claim, the matter is often resolved in a "walk away, everybody takes nothing" manner. In the debtor/creditor context, this means that when the creditor understands that you have legitimate claims for damages, and that the creditor is legally required to pay such damages, a settlement can be easily achieved. The creditor/collector, when presented with legitimate claims for violations of consumer protection laws, has to consider that even if the creditor wins the battle of collecting the debt, the creditor will ultimately lose the war, having to pay thousands of dollars in damages for their violations.

In order to prevail against your creditors and debt collectors, you must document and maintain evidence of your communications and efforts to resolve the creditor's claim. Once the debtor claims that the creditor/collector has violated the Fair Debt Collection Practices Act (FDCPA), a swearing match will ensue, whereby the creditor/collector will inevitably deny the alleged violations. It is critical that notes be maintained, that may be used later to refresh recollection of specific conversations and events that are relevant to the FDCPA claim. If you find yourself in a situation where creditors and debt collectors are undertaking to collect debts against you, you should immediately begin to collect evidence that may be later used in a civil proceeding.

# NECESSARY TOOLS FOR BATTLE

## Prepare Yourself!

It is necessary that proper evidence be gathered and preserved in order to prevail with respect to claims against creditors and debt collectors. Debt collectors spend thousands of dollars making sure they gather their evidence by tape recording phone calls and entering data into computer spreadsheets on each occasion that there is a contact made with a debtor. Likewise, it is imperative that proper evidence be gathered and maintained by the debtor, in order to convince a judge or jury in a subsequent proceeding that the creditor/collector is guilty of the alleged violations. Any person intending on prevailing against creditors/collectors should adopt the following procedures:

# Recording Phone Calls

- If legal in the State where you reside, a telephone handset equipped with a telephone recording device should be utilized to record conversations with the creditor/collector. Note: States vary in what is allowed with respect to recording phone conversations. Most states (35) and the District of Columbia allow conversations to be recorded as long as one person is aware that the call is being recorded. Other states (15) require that the other party be informed that the call is being recorded. (*You should consult with an attorney in your state with respect to your state law requirements.)* See Appendix A, which provides a summary of state regulations. *(Note: Laws change and you should only rely only upon advice of a local attorney. Be sure and follow your state's law!)*

## Free Phone Recording Resources

There are many free cell phone apps available that will record all calls. Some of the vendors of these programs offer paid versions that may have more comprehensive tools for recording. I personally prefer the App called "ACR." It is free and will record all incoming and outgoing calls, requiring that you monitor and delete calls that are not necessary to archive. Be careful of which App you choose. Some of them use the phone microphone to record and will only record your side of the conversation unless you have the speakerphone on. If you choose an App that has this drawback, keep looking for another one.

## Proof of Mailing

- Critical written correspondence to the creditor should be delivered via certified mail return receipt requested. Additionally, you should send a second copy of any such letter regular mail (not certified mail). This way, if you end up in court, and the recipient claims that he never received your letter, you can inform the judge that you sent it both certified mail and regular mail. If you then lack the recipient's signature on the green card (returned to you by the United States Postal Service), you may inform the Judge that you sent an additional copy regular mail, and it was not returned to you by the post office, which is presumptive that it was received. Most judges construe this type of mailing as "deemed received," even if the other party denies they received the mailing.

## Keep a Journal

- Keep a day timer or other chronological journal, so that you will have a record of each and every communication with the debt collector/creditor. You should keep this log available on each occasion you receive a call. If you have Caller ID, be sure and note all of the information from the Caller ID, including the telephone number where the call came from (even if the name reads "unavailable" or "out of area"). Obviously, you want to note the date and time of the call, the person you spoke with, and what was discussed. Finally, note the length of the call if your Caller ID shows such information. If not, estimate the length of the call in your journal.

## **Maintain YOUR FILE**

- It is essential that you keep copies of all information and communications received from the debt collector. This would include letters, e-mails, and voicemails. All of this information constitutes "your file." Remember, you only have to prove one violation of the Fair Debt Collection Practices Act to prevail. This violation could be in the form of an improper statement contained within a collection letter, a collection letter that omits required information, or a phone message in which the collector fails to follow required telephone protocol. Your file is the most critical information to prevail on an FDCPA claim. Also, if you are able to present such a file to an attorney who would consider filing an FDCPA lawsuit, the attorney will be much more inclined to make an immediate decision to take your case for free. Once you can establish even one violation of the FDCPA, you are legally entitled to $1,000.00 plus any and all other losses or damages, and your attorney recovers 100% of his or her attorney fees and costs. Likewise, having the evidence to present the claim will assist in causing the collector to dismiss its claims for the unpaid debt.

# PHONE PROTOCOL

## Be Professional!

- Remember when you are recording a phone call, that the call will likely be heard later by judge or jury, while trying to understand all aspects of your claim against the creditor/debt collector. It is important that someone listening to the call not perceive that you are trying to trap the creditor/collector, or that you are trying to bait the person on the other end of the phone into becoming uncivil or to commit misconduct. You should be nice and civil, irrespective of the behavior of the debt collector. Remember, the judge or jury will be sympathetic to you if you are the person who seems reasonable, and the one trying to conduct yourself in a civil professional manner. If you likewise engage in threats or uncivil attitude towards the debt collector, it may be perceived that you were not very emotionally distressed, given your aggressive conduct during the phone call. This does not mean that you should lie down and take abuse, without asserting your rights. You want to be clear in your demands that you be provided verification of the debt, and other matters that you will be requesting from the caller. Furthermore, you may be assertive in your demand that the debt collector "cease and desist" collection efforts, or that the collector stop calling at unreasonable hours or places, etc. You can assert your rights and present your demands in a professional way, but without sounding like you are getting satisfaction from the debt collector making threats. Likewise, you do not want to seem that you are making threats towards the collector.

- Many debt collectors will attempt to not let you speak. If this is the case, simply repeatedly urge your demands – that you be provided verification of the debt, that they cease and desist, etc. You are not required to endure inappropriate abuse. If it gets to that level, simply inform the caller that you are "hanging up now," and hang up. When your blood pressure rises during the call, remind yourself that the more abusive the collector chooses to be, the more likely you are to prevail in a FDCPA lawsuit and recover damages.
- If the opportunity presents itself, explain to the collector how phone calls are causing problems - at home, at work, with neighbors, etc. as may be applicable to your situation.
- If you dispute that you owe the debt, inform that you dispute the claim, and that you insist that the collector provide verification of the debt. "Verification" means documentation, as most consumer contracts are not enforceable unless in writing.
- If you are calling the creditor, and you are recording as permitted by the law of your State, verbally state on the recorder the date and time of the call before you press the last number to complete the call. That way there is no confusion when later listening to multiple phone calls as to when the call occurred. If the collector calls you, simply state the date time, phone number and where you are located (home, work, cell phone) on the tape after the call is complete.

- Do not provide personal information to the collector (i.e. place of employment, bank account locations, your social security number, driver's license information, etc.) You may respectfully tell the caller that you are not giving an interview, and that you do not provide personal information to people calling who are unknown to you. However, you should confirm that they are speaking to the right person.
- If the collector calls outside of the hours allowed under the FDCPA, state the time in the call to document yet another violation of the FDCPA. ("Why are you calling me at 11:00 o'clock at night?")
- Know who is on the phone: One of your first questions to the debt collector calling you should be "What is your fax number?" Follow-up questions should be "What is your name? Extension number? Name of your company? What state are you calling from? What is your address? On whose behalf are you collecting – for creditor? or do you (the collector) now own the debt? " When you meet with the attorney who is contemplating bringing a Fair Debt Collection Practices Act claim on your behalf, the attorney needs to know who it is he or she will be suing. Therefore, it is critical that you obtain basic identification information in each phone call. If the collector refuses to provide this information to you, the collector has just committed another violation of the FDCPA! Fax numbers are useful in sending your follow-up letters asserting your rights under federal law. It is very difficult for the Collector to later deny receipt of your fax, when the tape recording reveals that the collector verbally gave you the phone number to which you sent the fax.

- MOST IMPORTANTLY – Be sure and make the proper requests under the FDCPA. (i.e. Ask for the collector to provide you verification of the debt).

**Examples:**

**"I want a signed copy of the agreement you say I signed."**

**"Please send me all documents that you have that verify the debt."**

**"Please give me verification that I owe you the debt, including proof that you have the right to collect from me."**

**"Please identify your company (name, address, phone number, fax number)."**

# DON'T ADVANCE TOO QUICKLY!

When dealing with the creditor/debt collector, although the temptation is to immediately draw your sword and began battle, you should remember some basic concepts. If you come out of the gates claiming violations of the FDCPA too early, you will cause the creditor/collector to immediately refer their file over to their attorney, who will be very careful after you have threatened an FDCPA case. Much of the time, you can be placed at great advantage if you simply attempt to discuss the debt, and attempt to exchange some basic information that may be helpful to you at a later time. Those who engage in sports of hunting and fishing understand that you must lie in wait until it is the opportune moment to move in on your game or to "set the hook."

In most situations, it is not a good idea to immediately inform the creditor that you perceive that they are violating state or federal laws in their attempt to collect the debt. The better approach is to attempt to have conversation with them, requesting information about the situation. This gives the creditors the opportunity to comply with the law, or otherwise, to engage in prohibited conduct which you will document in your files and tape recordings (as permitted by law). For example, in conversing with the debt collector, you should ask questions such as the following:

**"I am not able to pay the debt because ________________"**

**"What are my options if I cannot pay the debt?"**

**"What will happen to me if I don't pay the debt?"**

**"What is the exact amount of the debt I owe?"**

**"I don't believe I owe this debt. What do I need to do to convince you of that?"**

**"Has this gone to a court judgment?"**

**"Will I get in trouble if I don't pay it? What can happen to me?"**

**"I don't have money to pay now. You will have to wait. Can you please work with me?"**

**"Is this something I should contact the original creditor to discuss?"**

**"What assets are you saying you can take from me if I don't pay this off?"**

**"Can I go to jail?"**

**"What is the law as it relates to this debt?"**

Inform them of the reason why you believe you do not owe the debt (i.e. "I believe I paid this debt." "The creditor charged off the debt." or "Isn't this debt too old to be collected?" – whichever may be applicable). Be sure and ask for information that the creditor/debt collector are required to disclose. Here are some examples:

> **"Who are you again? What is the name of your company? What is your address, phone number and fax number? What is your name and title? Do you have some paperwork you can send me to show me that I owe the debt? Do you have documents that I signed? Do you have the agreement that I signed? Can you send that to me?"**

Remember that all of the above questions are legitimate questions, inquiring of matters that you are entitled to know. Furthermore, by asking for this information, you are requesting for information that the debt collector is required to disclose. You are giving the honest debt collector an opportunity to explain matters that are important to you. At the same time, you are setting the trap for the dishonest debt collector who will stop at nothing to get money out of you.

Most attorneys who review potential Fair Debt Collection Practice Act claims will opt to wait and stay out of matters between the debtor and the debt collector until such time as a violation has occurred. If you advise the collector in the first communication that you are contending that the collector is violating the FDCPA, the collector will be much more careful and anticipate that you are gathering evidence to present a claim. Let the story play out before you leap and make claims against the debt collector. I use this tactic when I am taking an adverse witness's deposition or testimony in court. If I know the adverse witness is lying, I will allow him to lie over and over again, until he has buried himself so deep into the lies, that he cannot escape perjury once the lie is exposed. I will give him enough rope to hang himself by forcing him to address the issue in many different ways, such that by the time he leaves the witness stand, he has completely committed himself to his lying testimony. Then, when the truth is proven, he may be looking at prison time for his perjury. Remember, the goal is not to "set up" the collector. Rather, you are giving the debt collector time and opportunity to do the right thing, or to choose to do the wrong thing.

Once you have built a file with documented phone calls, letters to and from the debt collector, and perhaps tape recordings (if your State allows such tape recordings), it is time to formalize your claim that the debt collector has violated the FDCPA or other provision of law. Now you have the ammunition necessary to win the battle with evidence that supports your claim that the debt collector has violated federal or state law. Once you have the evidence that proves the violation, it is too late for the debt collector to undo the violation. At this point, you are ready to take on the debt collector with a more formal demand letter.

# Chapter 4

# DEFEATING THE DEBT COLLECTOR <u>BEFORE</u> THE WAR

By asserting your rights under the Fair Debt Collection Practices Act, and by carefully documenting and recording (as allowed) the conduct of the debt collector, you will find that you have won the war <u>before</u> any battle in the Courts. The most powerful of governments know that by employing pre-war tactics, that many battles may be entirely avoided without any war. The United States government has traditionally imposed economic sanctions as a tactic to eradicate the possibility of war against nations that depend on U.S. or other worldwide support. Strong governments understand that a conflict may be eliminated before battle though use of diplomacy and sanctions, for the simple reason that the opponent gains a clear understanding that even if it does well in certain advances, it will not be the ultimate prevailing party given the ultimate economic harm. An aggressive debt collector may be prevented from their goals of recovering money, by being caught in its own commission of unlawful acts.

More often than not, the collector will "close their file" and go away when it realizes that you have documented evidence of violations of the Fair Debt Collection Practices Act. Knowing that filing suit against you will prompt a countersuit against the collector for its violations of law, the collector will quite often elect to let the claim go, and pursue someone else.

## THE FAIR DEBT COLLECTION PRACTICES ACT (FDCPA)

The Fair Debt Collection Practices Act enumerates specific prohibitions, which are never allowed. Any one of the following requirements of law, if violated, amounts to a violation of the FDCPA. Remember, you only need to establish <u>one single violation</u> to prevail in FDCPA litigation, recovering monetary damages and attorney fees.[1]

The Fair Debt Collection Practices Act prohibits ***"a debt collector from communicating with a consumer in connection with a debt in any unusual time, place or at time and place known or should be known to be inconvenient for the consumer, unless the collector obtains the prior consent of the consumer or the express permission of the court."*** *15 U.S.C., Section 1692(a)(1).*

### <u>Time and Place of Communications</u>

- ✓ A debt collector may not call you earlier than 8 a.m. or later than 9 p.m. <u>in your time zone.</u> (It is not a defense for the creditor to say they called during the proper time where the collector was located.)
- ✓ The collector must honor the request by the consumer that the collector only communicate at certain times and locations. (i.e. If a consumer tells the collector only to call in the

---

1 The entire text of the Fair Debt Collection Practices Act (FDCPA) may be found at https://www.ftc.gov/enforcement/rules/rulemaking-regulatory-reform-proceedings/fair-debt-collection-practices-act-text.

evenings and only at the consumer's home, calling another place at another time is a violation.) This type of request does not have to be in writing, but can be made over the phone.

✓ Communication by the debt collector at the consumer's place of work is prohibited under the FDCPA, if the debt collector knows or has reason to know that the consumer's employer prohibits such communication at work. (The consumer simply needs to inform the debt collector that he or she is prohibited by the employer to accept any personal calls at work. A request over the phone is sufficient. This request need not be made in writing.) It is also sufficient if the employer, or any person at the workplace, has informed the debt collector that personal calls are not permitted.

**Examples of Evidence**

**"It is 10:00 PM my time. Why are you calling me so late?"**

**"Do not call me on my cell phone. I can only talk about this matter between 6:00 and 7:00 PM on my home telephone number."**

**"My employer does not allow me to receive personal calls at work. I have told you that the last three times you called."**

**"I told you on (date) to cease and desist all collection efforts. Why do you continue to call and harass?" (Inform of harm as may be applicable – i.e. my kids or sleeping, I have an ill parent living with me, I have a disability and it is hard for me to get to the phone, etc.)**

ALSO SEE: Sample First Response Letter to debt collectors attempt to collect debt, at Appendix C of this book.

## Communications with Third Parties

A debt collector is prohibited from communicating about the debt with any person other than the debtor who owes the debt, with specific limited exceptions.

- ✓ A debt collector may communicate with the debtor's attorney.
- ✓ The debt collector may communicate with a consumer reporting agency.
- ✓ The debt collector may communicate with the actual creditor, the attorney for the creditor or its own attorney.
- ✓ The debt collector may speak to the spouse of the person owing the debt.
- ✓ The debt collector may speak to a minor's parents, if the minor owes the debt.
  [Remember: States have laws that sometimes vary from the FDCPA with respect to communications by debt collectors with spouses and children. Also, most states' laws provide that minors are not competent to make contracts, and accordingly, an attempt to collect a debt from a minor that is barred by state law is a violation of state law, as well as a violation of the FDCPA.]

Serious problems exist for the debt collector when the collector leaves detailed information on an answering machine or in a voice mail. For example, if the collector says "My name is John Doe. I am with XYZ collection agency, and we are attempting to collect a debt from (consumer's name)," such message in and of itself is a violation of the FDCPA, if someone other than the

Debtor receives the message. Most collection agencies are aware of this problem, and particularly that their message is being recorded, and accordingly, they will either hang up, or leave a message such as "This is John Doe. I am calling for [name of Debtor]. Please call me back at 1-800-xx-xxxx." (Such a message does not violate the FDCPA.) However, you would be surprised that the number of inexperienced debt collectors who violate the FDCPA in their very first message left in voicemail, providing the consumer sufficient evidence to win a FDCPA case before even speaking to the collector.

# WHO CAN BE SUED?

## Debt Collectors

Debt collectors and collection agencies who work for a fee on behalf of a creditor, or another person or entity that has purchased the debt may be held liable under the FDCPA. This is true even if the debt collector has not been paid any fee, and is working on a basis where it will be paid a percentage of money collected.

## Lawyers and Their Firms

The Fair Debt Collections Practices Act (FDCPA) extends beyond debt collectors. Collection lawyers – that's right, **lawyers** – may also be held liable under the FDCPA. Law firms have been sued in class action cases as a result of their collection letters not meeting the requirements of the FDCPA. Interestingly, most attorneys representing consumers in FDCPA cases are not only interested in handling the one case that comes in their door, but the attorney knows that the FDCPA case may be brought as a class action case on behalf of every consumer who ever received the improper letter from the collection lawyer's firm!

Collection lawyers and their firms that violate the FDCPA are personally liable for damages to the consumer. Most law firm's collection efforts are actually handled by non-lawyer paralegals demanding payment on the debt. If a lawyer's paralegal misrepresents the account (i.e. holds himself out as a lawyer; demanding payment but does not review the creditor's claim sufficiently to be sure it is collectible), the law firm is liable under the FDCPA. Some of the largest collection law firms in the United States have been toppled as a result of simple violations of the FDCPA which resulted in a single consumer filing a case on behalf of himself and on behalf of "all persons similarly situated." This is known as a class action case, and is much easier to bring than other types of class action lawsuits. Some law firms have ended up themselves filing bankruptcy, or otherwise disbanding as a result of a bold consumer and his attorney filing the FDCPA lawsuit as a class action.

Collection attorneys, and their paralegal staff, are required to make clear disclosures in the first written communication to the consumer. Collection lawyers may not put their "spin" on this language, but must clearly and expressly provide required language informing consumers of their rights under the FDCPA. Such required language (commonly known as the **validation language**) is explained at other sections to follow in this book. Attorneys do not wish to be targets of an FDCPA law suit. For this reason, if an attorney threatens suit on a time-barred debt, or a debt that has other problems, he or she should be put on notice that in the event a suit is filed by the attorney's firm, that the attorney and his firm will be named as defendants in an FDCPA suit for attempting to collect an invalid debt. (See Sample FDCPA Letter to Attorneys at Appendix C-3 of this Book)

Studies of FDCPA litigations have revealed that juries are not sympathetic to collection lawyers who commit violations against consumers.

- ✓ Consumer sues Target and law firm collecting debt in New Mexico – $1.26 Million Verdict. (2011). Collector was pursuing the wrong person for the debt, and alleged an innocent error. The collector persisted with garnishments. The jury did not believe the creditor and spoke loudly with its verdict.
- ✓ Montana Jury awards $311,000.00 against debt collection law firm. The debt collection attorneys sued on the debt, but it was time barred by the statute of limitations. The jury found violation of the FDCPA for pursing a debt that was not valid. (2011).
- ✓ Oregon Jury awards $100,000.00 against collector who tried to collect on a credit card that was not the consumer's debt.
- ✓ Denver, Colorado – Jury awards considerable money damages against debt collector using abusive language in telling a stay-at-home mom to get a job.
- ✓ A Florida Jury awarded significant damages against a debt collector who failed to properly identity itself in a message on the consumer's answering machine.

- ✓ A California jury awarded $500,000.00 against debt collector caught on tape asserting that the account was legally owed when it was not collectable. (2009)

When the collection lawyer steps in to collect the debt on behalf of his or her client, you would be surprised at the number of FDCPA violations committed. Most lawyers are not trained about consumer protection laws in law school. Lawyers are, however, trained in law school to be aggressive and act as unwavering advocates for their client. The end result is that lawyers, being aggressive on behalf of their clients, routinely commit FDCPA violations. Once the violation occurs, it is actionable, irrespective of what the attorney may do to try to fix the problem. As they say, you cannot "un-ring the bell." Unlike other areas of law, the consumer does not need to prove what led to the violation, but rather, the consumer only needs to prove that a violation occurred. In many instances, the violation occurs in the form of a letter received by the consumer. The letter either fails to provide statutory validation language, or otherwise, the underlying debt is not a collectible debt. When this happens, there is next to 100% certainty that this same "cookie-cutter" letter has been sent to hundreds if not thousands of other consumers. This means a class action lawsuit against the law firm is warranted. Sending the lawyer a "red tag" letter[2] on the violation will assure that the lawyer never wants to hear from you again.

---

2 See sample Letter at Appendix C-3 of this book.

Below are examples of law firm letters which violate the FDCPA:

- Any collection letter that demands payment, but without providing all of the required FDCPA validation language (see below).
- Any collection letter that demands payment on a debt that is barred from recovery (i.e. the debt is too old and barred by the statute of limitations) without clear language that the debt is not legally collectable.
- A claim on behalf of a "debt buyer" that improperly alleges that the original collector is seeking to collect the debt, when that is not the case.
- A letter that demands interest and fees that are not specifically authorized by the contract that created the debt. ("You may owe other fees and costs." Lawyers love to use this broad language in their letters. It violates the FDCPA!)
- A letter that demands payment on a debt that may not be substantiated by documentation (debt buyers usually do not have the original documentation from the creditor from whom the debt was purchased). Such demands by attorneys have recently been the subject of challenges to foreclosure sales, where such demand letters were shown to have been "robo-signed", with low-level employees who had the job of signing affidavits to support debt collection judgments, when such employees had no responsibility to review or analyze the validity of the claims.)
- Recent court decisions have found that foreclosure law firms are subject to, and may be held liable under, the FDCPA.

### Check Collectors

Check collectors who offer services and attempts to collect dishonored checks may also be held liable under the FDCPA. These companies who seek to collect on bad checks must make all of the required disclosures in <u>all</u> communications to the person who wrote the bad check.

## Who is <u>not</u> likely going to be held liable under FDCPA?

The following groups of individuals and entities are not generally going to be liable under the FDCPA, although they may be liable for other violations of law in the process of collecting debts:

- ✓ The original Creditor is not governed by the FDCPA.
- ✓ Credit Counseling Agencies employed by the debtor are generally not governed by the FDCPA.
- ✓ County Prosecutor's Offices enforcing statutes that prohibit the consumer from delivering a bad check to receive goods or services.
- ✓ Child support collectors and state agencies seeking to enforce child support obligations.
- ✓ Credit Reporting Agencies – although such agencies may be liable under the Fair Credit Reporting Act (FCRA) or other state laws.
- ✓ Process servers serving litigation, although such process servers may be held liable for rendering false affidavits to

assist a debt collector litigant in securing an improper judgment.

**Important Provisions of the FDCPA**

- A debt collector must identify (name, address and phone) itself and the actual creditor.
- A debt collector must stop all collection efforts once informed in writing by the debtor to "cease and desist." (Any communication on the consumer's part that means the same thing as "cease and desist" is adequate to trigger the non-collection rule once demanded. The only choice that the collector has once ordered to "stop" by the Debtor is to file a lawsuit or go away forever.
- A collector may not identify that they are a collector, or make any reference to the debt to any person other than the Debtor. (Even leaving a message on your answering machine or voicemail is a violation if someone other than the Debtor retrieves the message – even if it is an immediate family member.)
- A debt collector may not threaten criminal prosecution.

# Chapter 5

## THE PREEMPTIVE STRIKE

"If we wait for threats to fully materialize, we will have waited too long." George W. Bush, Speech to WestPoint Academy Graduation Speech, June 2002.

Focusing on great military successes throughout history, governing lawmakers in the United States understood that the best way to assure military victory is to utilize the concept of preemptive strike. That is, war can be prevented if a preliminary preemptive action is undertaken before war begins. This doctrine of "preventative war" was one of the most controversial aspects of the George W. Bush Administration's foreign policy. According to the Bush administration, traditional techniques of containment and deterrence simply would not work when dealing with unstructured factions of terrorists intent on destroying the United States. The Administration declared that "the United States must be prepared to strike first." Although controversial, legal scholars and historians acknowledge that a preemptive force or strike on an imminent threat is most often very effective to defeat the objectives of the adversary.

Preemption, by definition, is the taking of action against a target when there is incontrovertible evidence that the target is about to initiate an attack. Taking action first against an imminent threat provides the strategic advantage of winning the war, in situations where going to war is inevitable, and where delay in attacking involves a greater degree of risk. In the context of dealing with the aggressive creditor, if it is abundantly clear that the creditor is about to file a lawsuit, destroy your credit and disable you from getting access to other credit, then it only makes sense that you strike first, to avoid getting hit with a judgment and losing credit standing. Once the creditor gets a judgment against you, it is very difficult, if not impossible, to defeat that creditor short of filing bankruptcy. The point I am making here is that if the creditor is telling you they are "about to sue you," then it is time to get aggressive with respect to your claims against the creditor. While it is important to raise defenses to the creditor's claim in response to a lawsuit, early leverage may be achieved if the borrower advances claims that the creditor violated state and/or federal laws through its conduct and practices. Once the lawsuit is filed, the collection lawyer has already agreed to see the case to judgment, as his fees have been contracted or paid. The creditor will be much more reluctant to back off the lawsuit, after its attorney has filed suit. However, early in the game, when the creditor/collector is deciding whether or not to send its file out to an attorney to seek a judgment, if the creditor has already been put on notice that the debtor intends to sue the creditor for violations of state and/or federal law (i.e. Fair Debt Collection Practices Act, Truth in Lending Act, State Deceptive Trade Practice Acts, etc.), the creditor/collector is much more likely to decide not to sue, and close its file.

Most creditors, debt collectors, and debt buyers make their decisions whether or not to spend money to file a lawsuit, based upon the perceived likelihood that they will recover money. Creditors understand that the great majority of collection lawsuits only last for a few weeks, <u>as 93.4% of the people sued on a debt</u>

won't hire a lawyer or even bother to answer the lawsuit. In such situations, the creditor wins whether the claim is valid or not, as the court will give them a default judgment. The cost in getting a default judgment against the debtor is minimal. Creditors/collectors understand that if they can garnish the paycheck even only one or two times, then they have recovered more money than it cost to pay the lawyer to file the lawsuit. Also, creditors and debt collectors often use attorneys who will file these lawsuits for free, based on expectation that they will get paid a contingent fee (often 40% to 50%) on any money collected. When creditors and their collectors decide to file a lawsuit, if they are in a situation where it costs them no money, what do you expect they will do? Of course, they will decide to file the lawsuit and seek the judgment. However, if the creditor/debt collector's file reflects that the consumer has placed the creditor/debt collector on notice that the consumer will be filing a counterclaim or other legal case for violation of state or federal law, the file is suddenly viewed very differently. The lawyer who agrees to take the case on a contingent fee percentage suddenly decides that he is in for a lot of work.

When lawyers work on a contingent fee (percentage of recovery), the fees don't go up when there are many additional hours of work. Also, attorneys working on a contingent fee will get paid nothing if they do not win the case for the creditor. Attorneys will decline to take a case on a contingent fee, no matter what the percentage is, when the attorney perceives many hours with an outcome of "low" or "no" dollars. I have often heard attorneys comment that "40% of nothing is nothing." Lawyers will not stay in business if they lose lawsuits, or if they expend hundreds of hours fighting a small claim, and end up with a percentage of a very small amount. Also, the contingent fee lawyers understand that even if they win the case, the defendant may take bankruptcy, and no money may be recovered. Likewise, if the creditor/debt collector is using an attorney who is paid by the hour, then the creditor/collector's bill can get very expensive, to the point where the attorney fees that have to be paid by the creditor/collector can exceed the amount of the total debt that they are trying to collect. Quite often, the creditor/collector will decide that it's not worth it to pay the amount of money it takes to get the judgment, especially knowing that even if they win, the defendant who now has a judgment against him or her can file bankruptcy and wipe the judgment away.

At the time a decision is made on the part of the creditor/debt collector to file a lawsuit, there will be a discussion between the attorney and the creditor/collector as to how the attorney's fees will be paid. The attorney will evaluate the complexity of the case (i.e. number of issues involved; Will there be counterclaims for alleged violations on the part of the creditor/collector?) to determine the amount of hours involved and the fees to be charged. If the attorney perceives that the case will involve a lot of hours, the attorney will usually refuse to accept the case on a contingency (percentage) fee. Likewise, if the attorney takes the case on an hourly fee basis, a much larger retainer will be requested from the creditor/collector, as there are additional issues that will have to be litigated beyond a simple complaint and default judgment. This makes the case much more expensive for the creditor/collector, and the likelihood is that the creditor/ collector will decide not to pursue the case, even if they believe they can win. No creditor wants an expensive collection case, as they already have great risk that the debt will never be collected.

In short, creditors undertake a risk-benefit analysis in deciding whether or not to sue on a debt. The benefit of the lawsuit is always questionable, since the consumer hit with a debt judgment will often file bankruptcy, and the creditor doesn't get paid. On the risk side, if the case is expensive and involves counterclaims and other issues, the creditor will most often decide not to sue, and let the debt go. By leveling a preemptive strike through certified letters noticing your intent to sue (or counterclaim against) the creditor/collector, you have placed matters into the creditor's file which will not be ignored at the time the creditor is deciding whether to sue and employ an attorney.

Taking preemptive action to assert your claims against creditors will often discourage the filing of any lawsuit. By undertaking such a preemptive strike, you may find that you have won the entire war against the creditor, without ever having to fight the battle.

# Chapter 6

## THE FAIR DEBT COLLECTION PRACTICES ACT (FDCPA)

The Fair Debt Collection Practices Act (FDCPA) was enacted by Congress in 1977 because of Congress's concern that there was ***"abundant evidence of the use of abusive, deceptive and unfair debt collection practices by many debt collectors which contributes to the number of personal bankruptcies, marital instability, losses of jobs and invasion of individual privacy."*** By passing the FDCPA, Congress intended to ***"eliminate abusive debt collection practices by debt collectors"*** and ***"to promote consistent state action to protect consumers against debt collection abuses."***

In order for the FDCPA to apply, the collection of the debt must be attempted by the "debt collector" against a "consumer." As stated earlier in this book, the FDCPA does not apply to the original creditor, but rather applies to debt collectors, attorneys, or other third parties who are trying to collect the debt for the creditor. The term also applies to a person who attempting to collect a purchased debt (the "Debt Buyer"). These are the players that will inevitably become involved in collection of the debt before a lawsuit is ever filed.

The term "debt" refers to any obligation of a consumer to pay money arising out of a transaction for "personal, family, or household purposes." It is important to note that the FDCPA does not protect debtors on business debts. The FDCPA protects a consumer owing a debt even under situations where the creditor may have secured a court judgment. Most importantly, the FDCPA provides protection to consumers who will be dealing with debt collectors before the lawsuit is ever filed. This is the time when the debt collector (who may even be an attorney) has its guard down, and will likely commit violations. Some violations may seem to some to be innocent and unintentional. Nevertheless, even a single violation of the FDCPA entitles you to recovery of damages and attorney fees. Proof of a single violation of the FDCPA allows the consumer to recover, even if the debt collector or the collection attorney made an innocent mistake. Ignorance of the law is no excuse, and you are entitled to recover damages. It does not matter that the consumer actually owes the debt. The debt collector must comply with the FDCPA in all respects.

Remember, if the consumer proves even one violation of the FDCPA, the consumer is entitled to statutory damages (minimum of $1,000.00) and entitled to collect any attorney fees of the consumer's attorney. Also, do not forget that only one violation of the FDCPA can be an act that entitles the consumer to file a class action lawsuit on behalf of thousands of other consumers who have been presented with the same violation on the part of the debt collector. One violation is all that is necessary to win a 100% favorable ruling from the court against the debt collector. Do you think the collector wants to face such a lawsuit, and the costs that it will have to pay to defend?

As you can see, it's very easy to prove a violation of the FDCPA. Upon establishing ***one single*** violation, the consumer is entitled to damages of the minimum of $1,000.00 statutory remedy, and any attorney handling the case is entitled to collect all of his or her attorney fees. In one recent 2016 case[3], an FDCPA case was decided by the jury on a $200.00 debt. The consumer, Lori Heling, found out that the court had entered a default judgment against her adding attorney fees and costs to the judgment bringing it up to $390.09. The debt collector obtained a wage garnishment, and when Ms. Heling called to discuss paying off the judgment with the collection agency informing that she never knew about the lawsuit, she was informed that "there was nothing she could do to have the judgment vacated." Ms. Heling found an attorney who sued claiming that telling Ms. Heling she could not seek to have the judgment set aside was misleading, and therefore violated the FDCPA. The jury awarded statutory damages to Ms. Heling, and the Court thereafter awarded attorney fees in the sum of $36,190.80. Notably, Ms. Heling did not end up having to pay the underlying debt, even though she may have lawfully owed it.

Debt collectors and their attorneys pay careful attention to end results like Ms. Heilig's case. This is why it is so important to take early preemptive action with an FDCPA letter and demand, preferably before the consumer gets sued. Debt collectors who routinely engage in illicit conduct will typically not take the chance of the consumer going to the FDCPA attorney and will likely go away if the claim is presented before they sue on the debt. Sample letters for all stages are at Appendix C of this Book.

---

[3] *Heling v. Creditors Collection Service Inc.* (Case No. 5-CV-1274, U.S.D.C., Eastern District of Wisconsin), 2016.

A complete copy of the text of the Fair Debt Collection Practices Act (FDCPA), in current form, may be viewed, downloaded and printed from the United States Federal Trade Commission (FTC) website. It is a relatively short straightforward statute. At time of publication, the URL (web address) for the text of the FDCPA is https://www.ftc.gov/system/files/documents/plain-language/fair-debt-collection-practices-act.pdf

Having a copy of the FACPA statute available enables you to quote provisions of the Act in your letters to debt collector and their attorneys to let them know you are knowledgeable of your rights, and that you possess the power and ability to respond to their efforts to collect the debt. Becoming well-versed in its provisions will carry you far in defeating creditors.

## THE RULES AND MANDATES OF DEBT COLLECTION

The following provisions are mandatory under the FDCPA. The debt collector or debt collection attorney does not have any discretion to deviate from these rules in any way. Violation of any of these rules – even one, constitutes a violation of the FDCPA, and grounds for a claim against the collector or the collection attorney.

### § 804. Acquisition of location information [15 USC 1692b]

Any debt collector communicating with **any person other than the consumer** for the purpose of acquiring location information about the consumer shall --

(1) **identify himself**, state that he is confirming or correcting location information concerning the consumer, **and, only if expressly requested, identify his employer;**

(2) **not** state that such consumer owes any debt;

(3) **not communicate** with any such person **more than once** unless requested to do so by such person or unless the debt collector reasonably believes that the earlier response of such person is erroneous or incomplete and that such person now has correct or complete location information;

(4) not communicate by post card;

(5) not use any language or symbol on any envelope or in the contents of any communication effected by the mails or telegram that indicates that the debt collector is in the debt collection business or that the communication relates to the collection of a debt; and

(6) after the debt collector knows the consumer is represented by an attorney with regard to the subject debt and has knowledge of, or can readily ascertain, such attorney's name and address, not communicate with any person other than that attorney, unless the attorney fails to respond within a reasonable period of time to the communication from the debt collector.

The FDCPA, at **15 U.S.C. Section 1692b**, specifically addresses how debt collectors and creditor's attorneys must conduct themselves when seeking information relating to the location and employment status of the consumer who owes the debt. The debt collector must specifically identify himself, but may not suggest in any way that he or she is attempting to collect a debt.

Also, the debt collector is limited in that they may inquire only one time. This is to prevent the debt collector from phoning again and again to an employer's place of business or to a family member for the purposes of simply seeking information concerning the debtor. Most often, alleging that the debt collector violated this provision of law is hard to prove, as it is a swearing match between the third-party (who usually you do not want to be involved) against the debt collector. Occasionally, a consumer debtor will be lucky enough to have a voicemail message, or other recorded message, which is useful in proving a violation of this section of the FDCPA. If a letter is ever mailed to a place of employment, even if it is addressed only to the debtor on the account, a violation of the FDCPA may be established. Debt collectors are simply not allowed to send collection letters to employers or other places other than the consumer's address provided in the credit application, or an address presented through credit bureaus.

The problem that debt collectors get into when trying to collect their debts by phone is that the FDCPA makes it mandatory that when the collector communicates with the person owing the debt, the collector must immediately advise ***"This is an attempt to collect a debt, and any information you provide will be used for such purpose."*** Lawmakers refer to this as the "***Mini-Miranda* Disclosure**." If the debt collector fails to inform of this information in the first written or oral communication, the collector has committed a violation of the FDCPA.

See **11 U.S.C. Section 1692e (11):**

**The following conduct is a violation:**

(11) "The failure to disclose in the **initial written communication** with the consumer and, in addition, if the initial communication with the consumer is oral, in that **initial oral communication**, that the debt collector **is attempting to collect a debt and that any information obtained will be used for that purpose**, and the failure to disclose in subsequent communications that the communication is from a debt collector."

Congress essentially required that with respect to <u>each and every</u> communication by debt collector to the consumer, the collector must inform that it is *"attempting to collect a debt, and any information obtained will be used for that purpose."* The big problem for the debt collector is that when someone other than the debtor answers the phone, the debt collector may not reveal that he is a debt collector, or anything about the debt. The debt collector is usually not aware of who the person is who answered the phone. If the person answering the phone is a roommate, a friend, or a family member, the debt collector may not disclose that he is calling to collect a debt. He may only ask to speak to the person owing the debt, and whether he has called the correct number. When the person on the other end of the phone asks, "What is the purpose of your call?," the collector may only state his name and phone number. He may not reveal the company that he works for, or why he is calling. Conversely, if the consumer owing the debt answers the phone, the debt collector *must* reveal specific information concerning his company and the debt, and give the required language that he is *"attempting to collect a debt, and any information obtained will be used for such purpose."* The dilemma for the debt collector, and where many violations are committed, is when the phone is answered by an answering machine, or the call goes to voicemail. The collector cannot leave this detailed information for the reason that someone other than the person owing the debt could receive the message. If a roommate, friend or family member retrieves the message, and the collector stated that he was attempting to collect a debt, a violation is committed. Likewise, if the debt collector does not leave this specific information, and the person owing the debt receives the message, the creditor has committed a violation by not providing this information. Debt collectors and their attorneys have long been debating about what is the solution. Most lawyers for debt collectors advise that the debt collector should leave no message at all, and just hang up. Other lawyers for debt collectors advise that a message should state *"This call is for John Jones. I need you to call us at the following number –"*

If you do receive voice messages from debt collectors, you should save the message, even if the collector only leaves a name and phone number. If you save this recording, you have enough to prove a violation of the FDCPA. As strange as it sounds, even a simple phone recording of the collector saying <u>anything</u> amounts to a "communication" by the collector, which imposes these mandatory requirements.

Recently, courts across the United States were confronted with the question of whether or not a recorded message by the debt collector sent to the debtor's home phone was a "communication" for FDCPA purposes. In one leading case out of

New York, *Foti v. NCO Financial Systems, Inc.*[4] the following recorded message was played and recorded on the consumer's answering machine:

**"Good day, we are calling from NCO Financial Systems regarding a personal business matter that requires your immediate attention. Please call back 1-866-701-1275 once again please call back, toll free, 1-866-701-1275, this not a solicitation."**

In the *Foti* case, the debt collector argued that the message was not a "communication" because it did not convey any information about the debt, and therefore, the message did not trigger the requirement that the debt collector identify itself as a debt collector. The Court held that pre-recorded messages were "communications" which mandated the requirements of the FDCPA. This Court relied on another California case[5], which recognized that a pre-recorded message, even if it did not convey any specific information, amounted to a communication. In that case, the message was as follows:

**"Hello, this is Thomas Hunt calling. Please have an adult contact me regarding some rather important information. This is not a sales call; however, regulations prevent me from leaving more details. You will want to contact me at 1-877-647-5945 as soon as possible. This is a toll-free number. Once again this is**

---

[4] *Foti v. NCO Financial Systems, Inc.*, 424 F.Supp. 2d 643 (S.D.N.Y. 2006)

[5] *Hosseinzadeh v. M.R.S. Assoc., Inc.*, 387 F. Supp. 2d 1104 (C.D. Cal 2005)

**Thomas Hunt calling and my number is 1-877-647-5945. Thank you."**

The California Court held that even though the message did not technically mention any specific information about the debt or even the nature of the call, it did convey information including the fact that there was an important matter that she should attend to and directions how to do so.

Courts reviewing this issue have held that the FDCPA contains "clear and unambiguous language" of Congress requiring disclosure in <u>all communications</u> by the debt collector. Such courts have held that if Congress wanted something different than a disclosure in all communications, Congress would need to rewrite this provision of the FDCPA.

The Mini-Miranda Disclosure must be included in not only the initial communication, but must also be stated in <u>each and every communication thereafter</u>. This includes <u>all written correspondence</u>. Using only words such as *"we are trying to collect this debt"* or stating that *"we are a debt collection agency"* is not enough to satisfy the Mini-Miranda Disclosure requirement. In addition to the Mini-Miranda Disclosure, any person attempting to collect a debt (including attorneys) must include other required language in written correspondence.

## Communication with Third Parties Prohibited

The Fair Debt Collection Practices Act prohibits a debt collector from communicating with any third party (person other than the debtor) regarding collection of a debt. Collectors may however to communicate with the debtor's attorney. Also, the collector is allowed to communicate to speak with the debtor's spouse regarding the debt, although some state laws prohibit talking to the spouse. The debt collector does not need to seek permission from the minor before speaking with a minor's parents regarding the minor child's debt. However, most state laws recognize that minors may not make contracts, and therefore, minors may not be held liable for debts. Any attempt to collect a debt from a minor in a state where a contract with a minor is void constitutes a violation of the FDCPA.

In a Florida case[6], the consumer contended that the debt collector left messages at his residence 11 times in the course of one year. The consumer alleged that his father, step-mother, step-mother's ex-spouse, girlfriend and neighbor all heard the message at different times. The message was as follows:

**"Hello. This message is for Thomas Berg. If you are not the person requested, disconnect this recording now. By continuing to listen to this recording you acknowledge you are the person requested. This is MAF Collection Services. We are expecting your call at 1-800-749-7710. This is an attempt to collect a debt. Any information obtained will be used for that purpose. 1-800-749-7710."**

In this call, the debt collector provided the Mini-Miranda language that "This is an attempt to collect a debt" and that "any information obtained will be used for that purpose." Furthermore, the collector instructed anyone other than Thomas

---

[6] *Berg v. Merchants*, 586 F.Supp.2d 1336 (S.D.Fla. 2008).

Berg to not continue to listen to the recording. The Florida Court held that it could be reasonably anticipated that someone other than the debtor would overhear the recording, and therefore, the collector violated the FDCPA. The Court also recognized that even if Thomas Berg was the one listening to the message, that others around him could be anticipated to overhear the recorded message.

The most important thing to remember is that if a debt collector leaves any message on a voice recorder, the message should be saved. Most likely, given the view of the court decisions on the subject, a voice message of any kind will likely violate the FDCPA. Remember, only one violation of the FDCPA needs to be shown for the consumer to be entitled to statutory damages and recovery of all costs and fees against the debt collector. Preserving your evidence is the key to defeating the debt collector.

## Stopping the Debt Collector from Calling at Work

The Fair Debt Collection Practices Act prohibits a debt collector from communicating with the consumer regarding the collection of a debt "**at the consumer's place of employment, if the debt collector knows or has reason to know that the consumer's employer prohibits the consumer from receiving such communication." 11 U.S.C. Section 1692c(3)** Essentially, Congress placed the burden on the consumer to inform the debt collector that his or her employer has a policy prohibiting phone calls from the collector at work. However, this is not a request that the consumer must make in writing. Simply verbally informing the debt collector over the phone not to call again because such phone calls violate the employer's company policy is adequate. Most the time, when the debt collector calls the consumer's place of employment, the collector knows that the phone call is not likely to be recorded. They will often continue to call, and later if asked, they will take the position that they were simply told "not to call at work," and that they were not informed that such phone calls were "prohibited by the employer." So remember, it is important to inform that phone calls from the collector are ***prohibited by the employer***. Since the person owing the debt is not usually able to record the phone call, it is helpful to have a co-worker (if you trust them) to witness you telling the caller that the employer prohibits calls such as these, and not to call again. This way, you have a witness who can verify that the collector was informed not to call again. If they do call again, a violation of the FDCPA has occurred, and the consumer is entitled to damages and all remedies under the FDCPA. Courts have severely punished debt collectors for contacting consumers at work: California (collector's threat to contact consumer's commanding officer violated FDCPA); Connecticut (continued phone calls to consumer at her place of employment, after collector have been asked to cease such calls because they inconvenienced the consumer violated the FDCPA); New York (sending collection letters to consumers employer violated the FDCPA); Missouri (damages awarded for multiple calls to place of employment threatening lawsuit after being told consumer could not accept calls at work); Arizona (Debt collector who continued to telephone employee at work found liable under the FDCPA).

# Times and Places that Debt Collectors May Not Call

The Fair Debt Collection Practices Act prohibits a debt collector from communicating with a consumer **"at any unusual time or place known or which should be known to be inconvenient to the consumer." 15 U.S.C. 1692c.** In addressing what times are appropriate for a debt collector to call, the FDCPA restricts the collector from calling "at <u>any</u> time <u>known or which should be known to be inconvenient</u>." Accordingly, should the consumer inform the debt collector that the consumer cannot receive calls during certain hours, the collector must honor this request. For example, if a person works the night shift, and is sleeping in the daytime hours until 3 o'clock in the afternoon, and it is made known to the collector that phone calls are inconvenient at any time prior to 3:00 P.M., the collector <u>must honor this request</u>. If the debtor informs that all times are inconvenient other than between 12:00 p.m. and 12:30 p.m., then the collector may not call at any other time other than this half-hour. The FDCPA provides that if the collector has no information about inconvenient times, that the collector shall assume that the convenient time is between 8:00 A.M. and 9:00 P.M. *local time* where the consumer is located. Interestingly, in the modern day of cell phone use, a person may receive a phone call on their cell phone and be located in a different time zone than their place of residence. If the creditor believes that a Texas resident is receiving a call at 9 o'clock in the morning, such call may actually be received at 4 o'clock in the morning if the consumer is on vacation in Hawaii. In such case, it would be important for the consumer to immediately inform "It's 4 o'clock in the morning where I am. It is not a convenient time to speak with you." If the collector persists in discussing the debt after receiving this information, he has violated the FDCPA.

As the FDCPA also prohibits the collector from communicating with a consumer at any unusual "place" known to be "inconvenient," the collector may be informed at the time of any call that the consumer is at a place where they cannot speak conveniently with the collector. If the collector disrespects the request for the collector not to call back while the consumer is at that location, and the collector calls again, the collector has violated the FDCPA.

Examples of Violation:

**Consumer**: "This is my mother's phone. This is not my home. I am here visiting. This is an inconvenient place to speak to you. Don't call me at this number again."

**Collector:** "Pay your debt and I won't call you here again."

Attempting to communicate about the debt after being advised that the collector has called an inconvenient place is a FDCPA violation. Any re-phoning of the consumer at the "unusual place known to be inconvenient," will amount to a further FDCPA violation.

Courts have already found that certain places are known to be inconvenient as a matter of law, such as a neighbor's home, a hospital or a funeral home. These are places that the collector should know are inconvenient. There have been cases where workplaces known to be inherently inconvenient would give rise to an FDCPA claim, even if the collector was not told by the consumer that the place was inconvenient. These places have included specific types of places of employment (i.e. nursing facilities, schools, factories employing assembly-line workers, and restaurants).

## Stopping All Phone Calls

There are two (2) situations where the debt collector violates the FDCPA by even placing one call. The first is the situation where the debt collector has been advised in writing by the consumer to stop calling. The second situation is where the consumer has advised the debt collector that he or she is represented by an attorney.

### Written Request to Cease All Communications

The FDCPA provides the tools necessary to completely stop all communications relating to collection of the debt. Most consumers do not realize that they can stop all of the phone calls and letters by simply making a written demand that the collector stop all further communications. Specifically, **11 U.S.C., Section 1692c(c),** provides as follows:

(c) CEASING COMMUNICATION. If a consumer notifies a debt collector **in writing** that the consumer **refuses to pay** a debt or that the consumer **wishes the debt collector to cease further communication** with the consumer, the debt collector shall not communicate further with the consumer with respect to such debt, except --

(1) to advise the consumer that the debt collector's further efforts are being terminated;

(2) to notify the consumer that the debt collector or creditor may invoke specified remedies which are ordinarily invoked by such debt collector or creditor; or

(3) where applicable, to notify the consumer that the debt collector or creditor intends to invoke a specified remedy.

The most important thing to note here is that the demand that the collector cease all communications must be in writing. In sending such communication, it is important to use U.S. Certified Mail Return Receipt Requested, and to keep a copy of the letter demanding that all communication cease. This way, the collector will have to sign the green card, which is proof of delivery and receipt by the United States Postal Service. (Note: While other methods are available for proof of delivery through the Postal Service and other delivery services, many courts still require the physical green card, which is why Certified Mail Return Receipt Requested is preferred proof of delivery if you will later need to prove delivery in a court of law. It is also a good idea to send another copy by regular U.S. Mail in case the collector refuses to sign for the certified letter. (See earlier Chapter on mail procedures)

Debt collectors are permitted to send you a basic communication after they receive your "cease and desist" letter, but such basic communication may be limited only to the matters set out in the statute. Normally, the debt collector will send one final closing letter advising that they will not undertake any further communication efforts. Normally, in such letter they will advise that they intend to pursue remedies under state law (i.e. filing of litigation in pursuit of court judgment). The bottom line is that the collector is prohibited from making any further phone calls to the debtor, family members, employers, anyone, after written notification to "cease and desist." If any phone calls or letters follow, even if the collector makes all the proper statements and disclosures, such additional communication will be in violation of the FDCPA. At this point, the collector has only two choices: (1) close their file and go away, or (2) file a lawsuit.

It is important to note that Congress also required debt collectors to stop communications where the collector is advised in writing that the consumer "***refuses to pay a debt***." This means that even a letter by the consumer to the debt collector that states that the consumer is disputing the debt, and therefore is refusing to pay, is enough to force the collector to stop communications. Any further communication after such a letter would violate the FDCPA.

## Informing of Representation by an Attorney

Debt collectors are prohibited from communicating with the consumer once they are informed that the consumer is represented by an attorney. This is true even if only the attorney's name is provided, provided that the attorney may be readily ascertained by the debt collector. Of course, the best way for the person owing the debt to communicate that they are represented by an attorney is to provide the name, address and phone number. Once notified, the debt collector may not communicate further, unless the attorney fails to respond within a "reasonable period of time" to a communication from the debt collector, or unless the attorney thereafter consents to direct communication with the consumer. In my law practice, I always had the procedure of allowing a client who was planning to file bankruptcy to set up their file in my law firm with a small deposit. Even though their bankruptcy case would not be filed for this initial deposit, the client would be urged to immediately inform that they were represented by me as their attorney. Clients would routinely inform that the calls would stop immediately. In fact, many clients followed up later informing that they might not even need to proceed with a bankruptcy filing, as they had not heard again from the debt collector or the creditor. While this is most effective, the debt collector will immediately make a phone call to the attorney, and if they are not clearly informed by the attorney that a representation exists, they will resume the process of debt collection. So, bluffing that you have an attorney does not work. The attorney must confirm the representation once contacted. Also, if the representation by the attorney is terminated, or if the attorney fails to respond to the collector's calls and letters, collection efforts may resume.

The most valuable attorney to retain to assist you in defense of a debt is one familiar with the provisions of the Fair Debt Collection Practices Act. If your attorney notifies that she has been retained, not just to defend a debt case or file a bankruptcy case, but also to evaluate the FDCPA violations, it is likely you will never hear from the collector again.

# MANDATORY DISCLOSURES UNDER FDCPA

**5 DAYS - The Creditor must Validate the Debt within 5 Days of the First Communication**

The FDCPA requires that the debt collector "validate" the debt no later than 5 days after the first communication with the consumer. This means that if you receive a phone call or letter of any kind from the debt collector as the "first communication," you should mark your calendar **5 days** from such communication. If this 5 day deadline passes without the debt collector providing the written Validation Notice, a violation of the FDCPA has occurred, and you are entitled to damages. If the Validation Notice is mailed timely, but the notice fails to state any one piece of the required information, a violation of the FDCPA has occurred. For this reason, it is important to keep any and all letters and collection notices received by mail. This includes keeping the envelope with the postmark. This information can be used to prove that the creditor did not timely mail the notice, or that the notice received within 5 days omitted essential information. If the debt collector is guilty of either problem, you have an FDCPA violation. Also remember that if the collection file gets passed over to a new collector, such as the attorney who has been hired to file a lawsuit, such attorney is also required to provide you the Validation Disclosure within 5 days of the his first communication. So many attorneys are focused on simply filing the lawsuit, or scaring the debtor through a letter that the lawsuit is coming, that they overlook the fact that they are also governed by the FDCPA. Also remember that if their first letter does not make proper disclosure that the attorney is "attempting to collect a debt, and that any information provided may be used for such purpose," that the violation of the FDCPA has occurred with the first letter. Even if the attorney provides this language, if a proper Validation Disclosure is not provided within 5 days, the attorney has violated the FDCPA.

**Required Contents of the Validation Disclosure**

At minimum, the Validation Disclosure provided within **five days** of the first communication must contain the following:

**The Collector Must State the Amount of the Debt**

**§1692g(a)(1)-**

**Within five days after the initial communication with a consumer, in connection with the collection of any debt, a debt collector shall... send the consumer a written notice containing –**

**(1) the amount of the debt;**

The FDCPA mandates that the initial 1692g letter set forth the "amount of the debt" along with other information. If the creditor fails to provide an appropriate disclosure of the amount of the debt, it has committed a violation of the FDCPA. While courts across the nation have issued different opinions, most courts have adopted the **"unsophisticated consumer"** test which assumes that the consumer is uninformed. For this reason, any statement that is confusing or misleading to an average person violates the law. In a case filed by a consumer against a law firm in Georgia, the court considered the following language set out in the collection lawyer's letter:

**The unpaid principal balance is $178,844.65. "This amount does not include accrued but unpaid interest, unpaid late charges, escrow advances or other charges for preservation and protection of the lender's interest in the property, as authorized by your loan agreement. The amount to reinstate or pay off your loan changes daily. You may call our office for complete reinstatement and payoff figures."**

The Court ruled that the letter violated the FDCPA, as the letter did not state an exact amount owed. The letter did not clearly explain the exact dollar amounts for the debt, interest, and attorney fees. The appellate judge deciding the case found for the consumer, indicating that the "amount of the debt" requirement of the FDCPA was "not met by providing the consumer with a phone number to call, nor is it an excuse that the accruing interest causes the amount of the debt change daily."

The bottom line is that the creditor's letter must state the exact amount due. It is fine for the debt collector to state that the balance may continue to accrue ongoing interest or attorney fees, as long as the exact amount due at the time of the letter is provided.

**The Collector Must State the Name of creditor to whom debt is owed.**

**§1692g(a)(2)-**

**Within five days after the initial communication with a consumer, in connection with the collection of any debt, a debt collector shall... send the consumer a written notice containing –**

**(2) the name of the creditor to whom the debt is owed;**

Most of the time, when a consumer is contacted by a debt collector, he is not properly informed that the debt has been sold by the original creditor to a "Debt Buyer." Debt buying has become a profitable industry, particularly in states that have very little protection to consumers. Most states permit wage garnishments to pay creditors judgments. Only a few states (Texas, Florida, and Pennsylvania) provide real protection from wage garnishments.

The Federal Trade Commission released a study in January 2013 which examined the structure and practices of the debt buying industry. Debt buying has become a rapidly growing industry. The FTC study determined that debt buyers typically pay no more than $.04 on every dollar of debt.[7] In other words a $5,000.00 credit card debt is purchased, on average, by a Debt Buyer for $200.00. The debt buyer knows that if it can get a court judgment and garnish the paycheck even one time, the Debt Buyer will make a profit. Realistically, the Debt Buyer will get more than one paycheck garnishment before a consumer will get organized enough to file Bankruptcy. Also, Debt Buyers understand that they can negotiate with the consumer to settle the debt for a reduced amount, and if the Debt Buyer makes any money above what was paid to by the debt, then the Debt Buyer will make a profit.

---

[7] Federal Trade Commission, *The Structure and Practices of the Debt Buying Industry* (January 2013).

There are no special rules that govern Debt Buyers. Debt Buyers are often more aggressive than the original creditor would be, for the reason that the Debt Buyer is in the game solely for profit, and not trying to avoid additional losses like the original creditor. When these accounts are purchased by the Debt Buyer from the creditor, they are purchasing the debts "as is," and usually will not have the credit history file that is necessary to give enough information to provide the required disclosures.

Debt Buyers must comply with the FDCPA, or they are liable for all damages and costs to the consumer. Debt Buyers must comply with the initial five-day disclosure requirement. This is often very difficult, if not impossible, for a Debt Buyer to do, as they usually do not have the necessary information in their file. This lack of information is your advantage in defeating the Debt Buyer in its attempt to get to your wages and assets. If you understand how to invoke your rights under the FDCPA, by demanding proper disclosures and verification of the debt, you have the advantage, and the Debt Buyer will often go away without you having to fight a lawsuit. In your letter to the Collector, always demand the identity of the original creditor and the identity (name, address, phone and fax number) of the entity that now owns the debt. (See Sample Letters at Appendix C)

Debt buyers are required to disclose the name of the original creditor, the original creditor's account number, the debtor's social security number, the date of last payment, and the date of charge-off. If a Debt Buyer is unable to furnish such information, it becomes impossible for them to meet the FDCPA requirement of furnishing an accurate statement of the debt owed. Failure to provide this information within five days of the initial communication is a FDCPA violation.

The following is an excerpt from the FTC's January 2013 Report:

**"[Debt] Buyers rarely received dispute history. Buyers rarely received any information from sellers concerning whether a consumer had disputed the debt or whether the disputed debt had been verified – information that would bear on whether the consumer being contacted owes the debt and whether the amount being collected is correct. Moreover, buyers often did not receive information that would allow them to break down the outstanding balance into principal, interest, and fees. The Commission has found that such information would assist consumers in determining if the amount of their debts is correct.**

**Buyers received few underlying documents about debts. Although buyers received the data file and some other information about the debts, as discussed above, they obtained very few documents related to the purchased debts at the time of sale or after purchase. For most portfolios, buyers did not receive any documents at the time of purchase. Only a small percentage of portfolios included documents, such as account statements or the terms and conditions of credit."**

Unless the consumer agrees with the amount alleged to be owed, it is always best to communicate that you **"dispute the validity of the debt,"** demanding that the Debt Buyer **"furnish proper verification of the debt and the exact amount alleged to be owed (including all calculations of interest, late fees, and other charges)"**. In its 2013 study, the Federal Trade Commission found that Debt Buyers rarely have the information required to disclose the exact amount owed, and are unable to breakdown the outstanding balance into principal, interest, and fees. This breakdown, necessary for a consumer to determine if the amount of the debt alleged is correct, is usually completely unavailable. If they cannot properly communicate the debt terms and amount owed, their collection attempts are prohibited by the FDCPA.

Some Debt Buyers have argued that they are not governed by the Fair Debt Collection Practices Act, as they are not a "debt collector." They urge that they "stand in the shoes" of the original creditor, since they now are collecting their own debt that they purchased. Since the FDCPA does not apply to original creditors, they argue that they are not covered. Courts finally settled this argument finding that the Debt Buyers are governed by the FDCPA. Accordingly, they must provide consumers all required disclosures, within five days after the initial contact. Failure to provide this information within five days of the first communication is a violation of the FDCPA, which means they owe you damages as a matter of Federal law.

**§1692g(a)(3) through (5) – The Collector Must Advise of Your Right to Dispute**

**Within five days after the initial communication with a consumer, in connection with the collection of any debt, a debt collector shall... send the consumer a written notice containing –**

**(3) a statement that unless the consumer, within thirty days after receipt of the notice, disputes the validity of the debt, or**

**any portion thereof, the debt will be assumed to be valid by the debt collector;**

**(4) a statement that if the consumer notifies the debt collector in writing within the thirty-day period that the debt, or any portion thereof, is disputed, the debt collector will obtain verification of the debt or a copy of a judgment against the consumer and a copy of such verification or judgment will be mailed to the consumer by the debt collector; and**

**(5) a statement that, upon the consumer's written request within the thirty-day period, the debt collector will provide the consumer with the name and address of the original creditor, if different from the current creditor.**

The "right to dispute" is one of the most powerful provisions of the Fair Debt Collection Practices Act. The Debt Collector is required to notify you in writing of these rights within five days after the initial communication. If the Debt Collector fails to provide you this exact disclosure in writing, or if the language in the Debt Collector/Attorney's letter does not accurately set forth the disclosures, an FDCPA violation has occurred. Secondly, if a the person receiving a proper notice of dispute of the debt, demands "verification of the debt" in writing within the thirty-day allowed, the collector has to <u>stop all collection efforts</u>. In fact, the debt collection attorney ***cannot even file a lawsuit***. Disputing the claim and requesting verification of the debt completely stops any collection or legal processes in furtherance of collecting the debt. If a lawsuit has already been filed, the attorney representing the debt collector may not proceed any further without first satisfying the additional requirements of "verification of the debt" under the FDCPA. Disputing the validity of the debt, and demanding verification is the key to stopping the process of collection in its tracks. Disputing the debt is as simple as notifying the Collector in writing of the following: **"I dispute the validity of the debt and demand verification. I request all information relevant to the debt, including the name and address of the original creditor."**

## OTHER VIOLATIONS (PROHIBITED CONDUCT)

Below are more examples of violations of the FDCPA, any one requiring that the debt collector fully compensate the consumer for all damages, costs and attorney fees, plus a $1,000.00 statutory penalty.

### Harassing, Oppressive, and Abusive Conduct Prohibited

The FDCPA prohibits any harassing, unfair, or deceptive collection practice. Congress did not specifically define what is meant by "abuse" or "harassment," but several courts have issued decisions that give us guidance.

### Collector Cannot Suggest that the Collector is Related to Law Enforcement

It is improper for the debt collector to suggest that the collector is somehow related to law enforcement. Examples that I have heard from clients in my practice are that debt collectors would refer to themselves as "Officer Jones," "Sergeant Jones," or "Lieutenant Jones." I have also heard of situations where the debt collector will inform the consumer of his "Badge Number."

Terms of this nature are deceptive, suggesting that the collector somehow related to law enforcement. Statements of this kind violate the FDCPA.

### The Collector Cannot Suggest a Crime or Threaten Criminal Prosecution

It is improper for the debt collector to suggest that a person will be criminally prosecuted. Many of my clients have told me that they were threatened by the collector that they would be "prosecuted to the full extent of the law." Some clients have informed that they were threatened that they would "be picked up," or that an "officer" will "show up" at their workplace. The debt collector would love to suggest that he was only referring to a process server who would serve legal papers. However, the courts use the "least sophisticated consumer" test in deciding how these threats are to be interpreted. Any language of this sort that would suggest criminal prosecution is improper. You should know that <u>you cannot be sent to jail or be criminally prosecuted for not paying a debt.</u> Suggesting otherwise is a violation of the Fair Debt Collection Practices Act. The United States does not have "debtor prisons." While a person may be jailed for failing to comply with a court order or for not filing required income tax returns, or for not complying with a court order to appear in court, they may not be jailed for inability to pay a debt. The only exceptions to this rule relate to nonpayment of child support and income tax evasion. Another improper tactic is to threaten that the debtor has "committed a federal fraud." Again, this is suggesting criminal conduct, and is a violation of the FDCPA.

## The Collector Cannot Make Improper Threats or Use Abusive Tactics

**"If you don't make a payment to me now, we will send someone to your work."** Even though a process server serving a civil suit might be permitted to serve the documents to a person at work, a threat of this nature is clearly for purposes of intimidation and coercion. Even threatening something that is legally permitted, if communicated in an abusive way, amounts to a violation of the FDCPA.

"**If you don't pay, we will call your work**." Even though calls at work are legally permitted, threatening to call a person's place of work in an abusive and forceful way is improper. Furthermore, it is already a violation if known to be an inconvenient place to contact the debtor, or if the collector has been advised that the employer does not allow such phone calls.

**"If you don't pay, we will call (any third party – your boss, your commanding officer, your neighbors, etc.)"** Threats to contact third parties are prohibited. An Ohio court found a violation of the FDCPA where a letter was written to a military serviceman to create the false impression that the collector would contact his commanding officer if he did not pay.

**"Pay now or we will call you every day for the next year."** Even though the FDCPA does not prohibit a phone call every day that complies with the FDCPA, to threaten to call every day is a communication that the collector will harass and inconvenience you if you don't pay. Threatening to call "every day" to harass and intimidate is a violation of the FDCPA.

### Threatening and Intimidating Language Violates the FDCPA

- Leaving telephone messages to consumer falsely stating that her social security number was under investigation. (New York Court)

- Large bold words **"FORTY-EIGHT HOUR NOTICE – WARNING – PAY THIS AMOUNT"** was found to be a violation of the FDCPA as the language suggested dire consequences would follow if the consumer did not pay immediately. (Oregon Court)

- Letter showing decapitated man and inquiring "Is this what you do with your head when you get our letters?" was threatening (Oregon Court)

- Printing at the top of a collection letter the acronym WWJD, which stood for "What Would Jesus Do?" had the effect of invoking shame or guilt by implying that the debtor was a sinner. The Court found the letter harassing, and in violation of the FDCPA. (Minnesota Court)

- Telephoning immediately after consumer hung up, inquiring whether she had a wedding ring, and a stating that she "should not have children if she could not afford the hospital bill" violated the FDCPA. (North Dakota Court)

- Collector that called the Debtor "a thief", telling her to "get a job" violated the FDCPA. (North Dakota Court)

- Racial stereotypes, belligerent threats, words like "liar," "deadbeat," and threats to ruin credit violated the FDCPA (Texas Court)

- A collector's letter threatening "extreme measures" and attaching an example of legal suit papers and sample court order for seizure of assets violated the FDCPA. (Federal Trade Commission Official Staff Commentary).

- The debt collector may not threaten to visit the consumer personally. (This implies violence.)

- It is a violation to threaten to publish in the paper or other media that the consumer is not paying his debts. (Threatening or using "Deadbeat Lists" or "Shame lists" are prohibited.) Some collectors have threatened to circulate free newspapers or publish online as some companies now do with people's mug shots. Collectors are only allowed to publish credit information through legitimate credit reporting agencies.

- Collectors may not publish delinquencies to other creditors. Likewise, they may not threaten to report to other creditors to try to harm the consumer with other creditor relationships.

- The Federal Trade Commission recently issued an opinion letter stating that that collectors could not circulate lists to merchants such as "check reporting systems," to encourage merchants not to take checks from the consumer. Doing so is a violation of the FDCPA.

## The Collector Must Properly Identify Itself

- Debt collector that uses an assumed name that is misleading or harassing – Examples: "Bounty Hunter Collectors," "U. S. Fraud Detection and Loss Recovery Bureau."

- A collection agency violates the FDCPA in using a lawyer's name. It is a violation of law for a debt collector to supervise an attorney, as the collector would be practicing law without a license. Even if the collector often uses an attorney, the collector may not imply that the attorney is involved or working on the matter, when that is not the case.

## Other Violations of the FDCPA

- Filing suit and obtaining a court judgment, after being notified that the debt was discharged in a bankruptcy case.

- Subpoenaing or otherwise informing a debtor that they must appear for a "debtor's exam" in an inconvenient or distant place.

- Attempting to seize Social Security or pension funds.

## Collectors May Not Abuse What They *Are* Allowed to Do under the FDCPA

- Although a collector can call the consumer, repeated or continuous telephone calls to annoy abuse or harassment are prohibited.

- Telephone calls must provide meaningful disclosure of identity. I have seen many situations, and even conferred personally with collectors on the phone who try to speak when I am speaking, absolutely refusing to give me their address and phone number. When asked to give this information, they will simply come back with another question, or complain that I am not letting them speak. Avoiding FDCPA required disclosures, and trying to shift the discussion to what the collector wants to talk about, is a violation of the FDCPA. Knowing that they are targets to FDCPA litigation, collectors will often try to tell you "I am a debt collector in Plano, Texas." Then, when you ask what is the name and address of your company, they will shift to something like "We are one of the collectors in North Texas handling one of your accounts." This "dodge and shift topic" technique is violates the FDCPA.

### Collectors May Not Misrepresent the Law or Cause Confusion, nor May They Provide "half-truths"

- Court punished debt collector that misrepresented state university's legal rights and obligations to withhold student transcripts.

- Court punished collector who informed that student loans would be revoked or made unavailable, such that the consumer would have to drop out of school, if the debt was not paid.

- It is illegal for the collector to say that he is calling from a "Legal Department," when no attorney is in their collection firm. If this happens, you should ask to immediately speak with the attorney. If they back-peddle and admit there is no attorney, or that the attorney is in "another office," the violation is established. If he says, there is no attorney, just a "legal department," the violation is established. If the call is transferred to the attorney, get the attorneys name and State Bar number.

- Court punished collector that suggested there would be additional collection charges and fees if another phone call was made. The original contract for the underlying debt did not provide for such charges.

- The debt collector may not suggest that there may be "fines" involved.

- Court found deception where debt collector suggested that it "could" sue, where the debt was time-barred. The debt collector argued that it could file the lawsuit, but would lose, and therefore it was not deceptive to say that it "could" sue. The Court found this half-truth to be a violation of the FDCPA.

- An allegation that the collector could harm the consumer's credit report, if not true – for example, if the debt was too old to be reported – amounts to a violation of the FDCPA.

- It is a violation of the FDCPA for the debt collector to threaten the consumer with a lawsuit, if the collector already knows it is not going to file a lawsuit.

- Misleading the consumer that the collector may have to "sell off the consumer's home and cars," where the state's homestead protection, and other legal exemptions, would not allow the collector to do so.

- It is improper for the debt collector to use a law firm letterhead, where the law firm has not been retained or involved in commencing formal proceedings. One court severely punished a law firm that allowed this type of letter to be mass-mailed by the collector, without any lawyer in the firm actually reviewing the consumer's file.

- It is improper for the debt collector to claim that it "has the federal government on its side."

- Using standard letters that claim "dishonesty," that are mailed out to all accounts that the collectors handling violates the FDCPA.

- Filing a lawsuit that is barred by law. (As I mentioned earlier in this book, it is statistically proven that 35% of all collection lawsuits are legally barred – either the debt is too old, or there is another valid legal defense that precludes the creditor/collector from winning a lawsuit.) Winning the lawsuit automatically entitles the consumer to recover damages under the FDCPA, as a Court has already determined that there was no basis for trying to collect the legally barred debt.

- It is a violation to use a letter that simulates a telegram creating a false sense of urgency.

- It is improper to suggest that a search of all of the consumer's assets has been instigated, when it has not.

- It is improper to suggest that a payment will improve the consumer's credit rating.

- It is improper to attempt to collect a debt that the consumer already settled with the creditor.

- It is improper to make confusing statements about the amount to pay off or to settle the debt.

- It is improper to misrepresent that the collector has verified the consumer's employment.

- It is improper to impersonate a lawyer.

- It is improper to misrepresent that numerous other communications had occurred between the collection agency and the consumer, when in fact it had not. These agencies love to use their "cookie cutter" form letters that say the same to every consumer who receives them. The standard forms can get the creditor into big problems under the FDCPA.

- It is improper to impersonate another person by using a caller ID spooling service. These devices give false caller ID numbers, or otherwise represent the call is coming from an official location or origin. Have you ever received a call from 000-000-0000? Trust me, it doesn't exist!

- It is improper to present a deceptive settlement offer. In one case, the creditor had authorized the collector to give the debtor a 30% discount "at any time," yet the collector informed the debtor that they only had a very short time to accept such an offer. Leading the consumer to believe that the offer was a "limited time offer," when such was not the case was deceptive, and a violation of the FDCPA.

- In one case, a collection letter that falsely communicated that the creditor's initial settlement offer was a "final offer," when such was not the case. This false letter amounted to an FDCPA violation.

- Serving legal documents on a consumer who is not represented by an attorney in ongoing court proceedings, and explaining the effect of such documents in a misleading way is a violation of the FDCPA.

- Faking up documents such as credit card statements or ledgers of charges by the collection company, to attempt to satisfy the validation requirement is a violation of the FDCPA.

- Filing a false affidavit attached to a debt collection lawsuit violates the FDCPA.

- Requesting a court to enter a judgment by default based upon a misleading allegation that the consumer is not responding to formal requests for information violates FDCPA.

- Attempting to garnish wages for an amount that is not supported by the judgment violates FDCPA.

- A debt collector may not falsely imply affiliation with the government.

The above list is not a comprehensive list. The key thing to remember is that <u>any false or misleading statement</u> by the debt collector, whether intentional or not, violates the Fair Debt Collection Practices Act. (Remember Ms. Helings case at Page 73 of this book?) Again, it only takes one violation of the FDCPA to entitle the consumer to recover statutory damages, all losses and damages suffered, court costs and attorney fees. And as previously mentioned, if one violation is spotted in a letter, the attorney handling the FDCPA case can ask the court to certify the case as a class action case, which means that now the debt collector is being sued for the entire class of consumers who have received the letter. You can imagine the expensive fees and costs that the debt collector will incur in fighting thousands of claims that were brought about by one single consumer. It is this power that is within the consumer's reach that will topple the debt collector, holding it accountable for its illegal conduct. As previously mentioned, where a debt is at issue, in many cases, the creditor/collector would be insane not to forgive the debt and walk away. In this situation, it is common that the creditor/collector is the one begging for the lawsuit to be dismissed with everyone walking away.

## WRITTEN NOTICE OF DISPUTE OF THE DEBT STOPS ALL COLLECTIONS, EVEN LAWSUITS

**§ 809. Validation of debts [15 USC 1692g]**

**(b) If the consumer notifies the debt collector in writing within the thirty-day period described in subsection (a) that the debt, or any portion thereof, is disputed, or that the consumer requests the name and address of the original creditor, the debt collector shall cease collection of the debt, or any disputed portion thereof, until the debt collector obtains verification of the debt or any copy of a judgment, or the name and address of the original creditor, and a copy of such verification or judgment,**

**or name and address of the original creditor, is mailed to the consumer by the debt collector.**

**(c) The failure of a consumer to dispute the validity of a debt under this section may not be construed by any court as an admission of liability by the consumer.**

If you notify the debt collector, in writing, within thirty days after the collector notifies it is collecting a debt, that the debt is disputed, the entire collection process is brought to a halt. A collection lawsuit may not proceed. No more communications may occur by phone or in writing. Yes that's right, the collection process completely ends! Also, even in situations where the debt is not disputed, should you notify the debt collector, in writing, that you are requesting the name and address of the original creditor, the collection process must stop. Again, this is a process that will stop the collector in its tracks, provided that the notice and request are presented **in writing.** Although it doesn't hurt to tell the collector over the phone that you "dispute the debt," until you communicate this information in writing, the provisions of 11 U.S.C., Section 1692(g) do not go into effect. This provision provides that the collector must furnish "a copy of the judgment, or the name and address of the original creditor, and a copy of such verification or judgment, or name of the original creditor," to be mailed to the consumer. Unless and until you receive this information by mail from the collector, the process of collection is over.

Once this written notice is provided, it is incumbent upon the collector to furnish the required information by mail. If you receive any other collection demands (i.e. invoices, letters requesting payment on the debt, or lawsuit papers served upon you) and the collector has not mailed this information, an FDCPA violation has occurred. As mentioned before, only <u>one violation</u> of the FDCPA is required for the consumer to recover damages from the collector.

If you fail to notify the debt collector, in writing, within the thirty-day period, you may still notify the debt collector later that you "dispute the debt," and that you are requesting information (name and address) regarding the original creditor. You will still place into effect the protections of the FDCPA even though the thirty days has expired. The fact that thirty days has already passed simply means that the creditor/collector may now assume that you have sufficient information regarding the debt, and that you do not dispute the debt, in moving forward with litigation in the courts. Disputing the debt after the thirty days has passed will still force the collector to end its collection process. Remember, provisions of the FDCPA discussed earlier require that the collector "cease and desist," once you inform them in writing that you dispute the debt, or that you demand that collection efforts stop. Once you have formally advised the collector in writing that you dispute the debt or to stop collection efforts, they only have two choices under the law: (1) go away and close their file, or (2) sue you.

It is always best to respond to the first written demand for payment, advising that you dispute the debt and request verification. I usually believe it benefits my clients to demand copies of the transactional documents (credit card agreement, signatures of the debtor, copies of charge receipts evidencing the separate individual purchase transactions, all communications from the original creditor to the debtor). As previously explained, in most situations the debt has been purchased by a Debt Buyer, and this information is not available. Properly responding in writing to the collection efforts of a debt collector will most often result in the matter going away forever. Sample letters are provided at the end of this book (The War Chest).

## DAMAGES THAT MAY BE RECOVERED UNDER FDCPA

In order to prevail on a FDCPA claim, it is necessary only to prove one single violation. If that one violation is established, the consumer is entitled to recover damages. If the violation is of a type that has occurred with many other consumers (i.e. improper language in a collection letter), then the case may be filed as a Class Action, on behalf of the consumer, and all other consumers similarly situated (this can be literally hundreds of thousands of people). If the court finds a violation, the following damages are awardable:

1. **Statutory damages** in the sum of $1,000.00 for the consumer.

2. All **actual damages** to compensate for humiliation, embarrassment, mental anguish or emotional distress. (There is <u>no limit on the amount of damages that may be awarded.)</u>

3. **Punitive damages** – Punitive damages (damages to punish the collector and to set an example to other collectors) are additional damages that the court or jury may decide should be awarded to punish the debt collector and to make an example to

others. There is no set limit on the amount of punitive damages. Courts and juries can award millions of dollars, depending on the severity of the violations.

4. **Attorney fees** and **costs** of the litigation. (This is why the consumer can find a lawyer who will work for free with the expectation to be paid by the debt collector after a favorable judgment is received.)

5. **Class Action Damages**: Up to $1,000.00 per consumer for each named class member, plus up to $500,000.00 or 1% of the debt collector's net worth, whichever is less.

You can see why debt collectors and Debt Buyers do not want to get sued for alleged violations of the Fair Debt Collections Practices Act. Don't forget that the collector also has to pay its attorney to defend the case which can run in the hundreds of thousands of dollars. Also, the creditor/collector has to be mindful that publicity may be drawn to the case. Members of the public may become aware of the illegal practices, and many other lawsuits may follow. If a consumer's attorney is trying to make the case into a class action, the attorney may take out advertising, Internet websites, TV commercials, or other means to get the word out that other people may have a claim. This is the last thing that the creditor/debt collector wants to see happen. The creditor/debt collector has great incentive to want to settle the case, or otherwise make the FDCPA claim go away. Such is the reason why the consumer has great power to defeat the creditor/collector with respect to its claims. In most instances, if a violation of the FDCPA may be established, the creditor/collector will offer to dismiss its claim for the debt in its entirety.

Third parties (people who do not owe the debt, but who are harassed, or who are forced to deal with the debt collector) may also recover damages for the debt collector's conduct towards them.

# Chapter 7

# The Truth in Lending Act (TILA)

"I am a firm believer in the people. If given the truth, they can be depended upon to meet any national crisis. The great point is to bring them the real facts." *Abraham Lincoln*

The Truth in Lending Act (TILA) was passed in 1968, after many years of study on the part of the United States Congress. President Lyndon B. Johnson signed the Consumer Credit Protection Act (CCPA) which contained the Truth in Lending Act (TILA) as its first subpart. Many states have also passed their own version of the Truth in Lending Act, requiring even more disclosures and consumer information within contracts and finance documents.

The main goal of TILA was to require creditors to provide a number of disclosures to consumers at the time the consumer signed the creditor's contract. TILA compelled creditors extending credit to consumers to disclose "the cost of credit" (finance charges) in a standardized format and using mandated language. This information must be provided to the consumer at the time that the consumer signs the contract or agreement. The law requires that specific information be given to the consumer on the actual contract or note, on the same side of the page or on one side of a separate disclosure document. TILA is aimed at arming the consumer with specific information relating to the cost of credit, in order that consumers may compare terms of the financing with proposals from other creditors who are offering the same type of financing. The TILA also gives consumers certain rights to cancel certain contracts within a specified time after signing the contract. (Three-day cancellation rights on certain secured loans). This is known as Regulation Z.

The whole idea of TILA was to raise the level of consumer awareness as to the terms of their contracts. Congress wanted to prevent creditors from hiding the ball through use of fine print, or reference to another document. Congress understood that creditors' contracts presented a situation of "information overload" to consumers, such that the law would need to provide mandatory rules requiring disclosure and information. In 1988, Congress added the Fair Credit Card and Charge Card Disclosure Act to the TILA, as Congress understood the consumers were being bombarded with credit card solicitations. In Senate hearings it was estimated that consumers received over **two trillion** credit card solicitations in 1987. Congress acknowledged that consumers were not being given adequate information regarding the terms of their credit cards, and that some of the disclosures were not even made by the card issuer until after the consumer received the credit card. Also in 1988, Congress added the Home Equity Loan Consumer Protection Act of 1988, which dealt with home equity loans. Such provisions were passed to deal with abusive mortgage practices perceived by Congress. This legislation was designed to prohibit lenders from steering consumers into mortgage loans that were not in the consumer's best interest in order to increase the commission that would be paid to the loan originator.

Violation of the Truth in Lending Act entitles a consumer to recover statutory damages, costs of litigation, and attorney fees. However, the most powerful remedy created by TILA was the right to rescind the contract. In a mortgage situation, if the mortgage lender violates TILA, by failing to provide proper disclosures, or is found to have misled the consumer with respect to the transaction, the consumer now has the power to rescind the entire transaction. Rescission would result in the security agreement (mortgage) being voided, forcing the lender to release any Deed of Trust or Mortgage from the property, which would modify the lenders status from secured to unsecured, eliminating the possibility of any foreclosure.

TILA demands strict compliance. A violation of TILA can result in the creditor completely losing its lien on a home or vehicle. Although the TILA gives powerful rights to consumers, the act has been amended in recent years, easing the penalties to creditors for violations, such that they will be penalized only for "significant" violations.

TILA also provides for criminal prosecution for willful violations. TILA prohibits bait and switch advertising of credit terms (creditors offering credit terms in their advertising, when such terms are, in fact, not available). TILA also provides for resolution procedures for credit card billing disputes. Creditors are required to inform of consumer dispute procedures when the account is opened. TILA regulates leases of personal property (rent to own contracts) that extend for more than four months. TILA regulates disclosures that must be made in connection with student loans. TILA regulates the credit card industry by imposing required disclosures, at the time of the initial credit card agreement, and at intervals thereafter. TILA prohibits a creditor from communicating an interest rate (Annual Percentage Rate - APR) in an advertisement or document to attract the consumer, and then providing different terms in the actual credit agreement.

The Truth in Lending Act should not be overlooked as a defensive weapon in responding to a creditor's attempt to collect upon its contract. Although creditors try to be very careful in complying with TILA by having their lawyers draft and approve language in their contracts, should a TILA violation occur, the creditor is exposed to tremendous liability. If the creditor fails to properly disclose information within the contract, or if the creditor fails to provide appropriate disclosures in advance of having the consumer sign the contract, it has not only committed one violation, but has committed a violation with respect to many thousands of other consumers who also received the same paperwork in obtaining the credit. A creditor who has committed a TILA violation knows that the consumer need only place one phone call to a law firm that handles consumer class action litigation, and they will be facing a lawsuit brought on behalf of many thousands of consumers, which can cost the creditor millions of dollars in defending in resolving claims for everyone affected. The prudent creditor who has failed to disclose properly will not want to take the chance of having a consumer ignite the process of a class action suit. They know that there are class action attorneys waiting by the phone for a consumer to call with a TILA violation.

## Preparing the TILA Violation Claim

In order to successfully assert a TILA violation claim, you need to retain all documentation that has anything to do with the transaction. This includes any advertisements, webpage printouts, email solicitations, brochures, written disclosures and loan documents. Any time you enter into a significant loan transaction, such as purchasing a car or incurring credit, you should create a file that contains every single document you have ever received in connection with the transaction. Also, it is important to retain the original document. The original document is necessary to prove the size of the print, whether or not certain items were stated in bold language, and whether or not the creditor placed the significant language on a separate page versus the backside of the document. Also, if you end up in court, some courts will require the original document, and will prevent a witness from testifying as to the description of the document under the Best Evidence Rule.

TILA violations occur as a result of failure or neglect on the part of the creditor to provide information in writing. TILA does not involve conduct on the part of collectors when the debt is in default like the Fair Debt Collection Practices Act. Judges usually can decide whether or not TILA violations have occurred by reviewing the consumer contract, advertisement and disclosures that you will collect as part of your file on the creditor.

Examples of TILA Coverage and Violations

- Ford Motor Credit sued the consumer in the Municipal Court for $2,658.00 after the consumer turned in his leased car, stating that the charges were for "excessive wear and use." The lease stated that the consumer "may be charged for excessive wear based on our standards for normal use." The consumer responded with a counterclaim asserting, among other claims, that the creditor violated provisions of TILA (Consumer Leasing Act provision). The case was transferred to the Federal Court, where the consumer requested the court to certify the case as a class action for other consumers who were hit with such undisclosed charges.

- Basic interest costs not being properly disclosed (Tennessee court found violation in creditor contract that stated, "Note that this does not include additional interest fees that accrue after the loan closing, due to late payments under a daily interest calculation.")
- Disclosure of a finance charge greater than permitted by state law violates TILA.
- "Add-on fees" constitute finance charges, and if not properly disclosed, violate TILA.
- Overdraft charges on checking accounts constitute finance charges, as the consumer is charged for use of credit in situations where the bank advances funds. TILA disclosures must be provided in advance of charging such fees.

- "Courier expense" charges in mortgage loan closing transactions must be disclosed as part of the financing fees.

- Credit card "annual fees" must be disclosed as a cost of credit at the time of the initial consumer transaction, and before charges are incurred by the consumer.

- Fees paid to mortgage brokers directly from the lender, described as "yield spread premiums" are part of the cost of lending and must be disclosed under TILA. Application fees, discount fees, underwriting fees, and loan origination fees must also be properly disclosed in real estate financing.

- Late charges that are anticipated at the time of contract. "You may pay off the balance after 30 days, but any unpaid balance after 30 days shall be subject to a late fee of 1.5% per month." A creditor charging in this manner must make all TILA disclosures, which include large bold print as to the finance charge that is bigger than any other word in the document.

- Credit Life Insurance sold at the time of the credit transaction, but paid over a set term may be a financed transaction requiring TILA disclosures.

- GAP Insurance financed within a car loan must include disclosures required under TILA.

## TILA Required Disclosures

The disclosures that are required under the Truth in Lending Act depend on the type of financing that is involved. TILA distinguishes between "Closed-end Credit Disclosures" and "Open-end Credit Disclosures." A "closed-end" credit account is one where the consumer cannot continue to make ongoing charges. An example of a closed-end credit account is an automobile loan or a principal mortgage loan. An "open-end" credit account is one that is open and available for ongoing charges to be made by the consumer. Examples are credit cards, retail charge accounts, and home-equity lines of credit. Open end credit accounts contemplate repeated transactions, which can involve changes in finance charges and terms of the credit account over time.

## Closed-end Credit Disclosures

Required disclosures must be <u>conspicuous and clear</u>. "Conspicuous" means the disclosure must draw the consumer's attention. "Clear" means "not misleading or capable of more than one interpretation." The following disclosures are required in closed-end contracts:

- The finance charge must be more conspicuous than any other required disclosure, other than the creditor's name and address. This means that there may be no print larger than the then the disclosed finance charge.

- Finance charges must be disclosed in the form of APR (annual percentage rate). A description of the annual percentage rate must also be provided. This disclosure also must be more conspicuous than any other required disclosure.

- The payment schedule must include the dollar amount of the payments.
- The creditor must disclose the number of payments needed to pay the originally scheduled transaction.
- The creditor must disclose the timing of payments (due dates).
- The "total of payments" must be disclosed, and a brief description of the total of payments must also be provided. If the loan is for a mortgage made after January 30, 2011, the total of payments will no longer be required, nor will a schedule be necessary.
- The creditor must disclose whether it has or will acquire a security interest (lien) in the property being purchased or with respect to other property. Creditors may use the words "pledge," "lien," "mortgage" or other similar term.
- The identity of the creditor must be disclosed. (Only the name of the creditor is required. Premiums for credit life insurance, credit disability insurance, and credit property insurance, if included in the finance charges, must be properly disclosed.)

## Open-end Credit Disclosures

Open-end credit disclosures include credit cards, retail accounts, and home equity lines of credit. Special concerns exist with respect to these accounts, as consumers may be trapped with balances they can't pay off, and therefore unable to avoid imposition of increased finance charges, when the consumer is only able to make minimum payments. Open-end credit accounts covered by the TILA are those that require more than four installments. Disclosures required with respect to "open end credit" accounts included the following:

- Finance charges must be explained by annual percentage rate (APR), with explanation of calculation.
- "Promotional rate" disclosures require the creditor to use the word "introductory," when offering an introductory APR. Creditors must disclose when the a promotional interest rate (i.e. "zero interest for six months") will end, as well as the post-promotional APR that will apply after the promotional period expires.
- "Deferred interest" programs (credit card accounts that provide no interest until a certain day, but then retroactively assess interest charges from the purchase date if the consumer does not pay off the full balance) must include sufficient information so that the consumer understands the interest calculations if the balance is not paid by the promotional deadline. The creditor must state very conspicuously that "zero interest does not apply if the balance is not paid in full by the deadline."

- Annual fees must be disclosed in clear and conspicuous language.
- Late payment, over-the-limit fees, and return payment fees must be disclosed.
- Detailed required disclosures must be made over the phone if the creditor takes a telephone application.
- Required written disclosures must be made before the first charge on the open-end account. Creditors are required to disclose the method of computing the balance on which the finance charges will be calculated.
- Creditors must disclose information about the consumer's right to dispute transactions. Additionally, if the credit card issuer imposes charges for unauthorized use of credit cards, it must notify the cardholder.
- A periodic billing statement must be sent to the customer at the end of each billing cycle, if either a finance charge has been imposed, or there is an outstanding balance of more than $1.00. If no amount is owed, then no statement needs to be sent.
- Account statements must be mailed no later than twenty-one days before the due date. No late penalties or finance charges may be charged within this twenty-one day period.
- An address must be provided to which the consumer may send billing error notices.

- In at least one billing cycle per year, a statement advising of legal protections for billing errors, as well as claims and defenses available to credit card users must be provided.

- Any change of finance charges or fees on the open account must be communicated in writing not less than forty-five days before such changes take effect.

A creditor who violates TILA requirements is liable for actual damages, statutory damages and attorney fees. Statutory damages are based upon twice the amount of finance charges not properly disclosed, not to exceed $5,000.00. Lawsuits under the TILA may be brought as a class action, for the benefit of all consumers who were denied proper disclosures under TILA. Again, this is a situation where the consumer may benefit in defending a collection lawsuit, by informing the creditor that the consumer intends to pursue a TILA violation case and seek class action certification, should the creditor not resolve claims in a mutually agreeable manner.

The requirements of the Truth in Lending Act are much too vast and comprehensive to fully cover in this publication, without causing information overload to the reader. Much information as to the details of required TILA disclosures is available on the Federal Trade Commission and United States Consumer Financial Protection Bureau websites.

# Chapter 8

## DEFEATING THE COLLECTION LAWSUIT

"No matter how long it may take us to overcome this premeditated invasion, the American people in their righteous might will win through to absolute victory." Franklin Delano Roosevelt, Speech to the Congress the day after the attack on Pearl Harbor. Dec. 8, 1941.

In the event that a debt collector files a lawsuit against you, there are specific defenses that must be raised timely and appropriately in order to defeat the litigation. In the event that claims against the debt collector are not properly and timely asserted, such matters are waived. Also, just like the creditor must present its claim timely in court, you must also assert your claims under the Fair Debt Collection Practices Act and other provisions of law. The Fair Debt Collection Practices Act (FDCPA) requires that you file suit in a court of competent jurisdiction, no later than one year after the event alleged to have violated the FDCPA. In the event that you are sued, you have responsibilities to timely assert any counterclaim or defense to the lawsuit, and if you fail to do so properly, such matters are deemed waived.

The purpose of this Chapter is to effectively equip the reader to fight the collection lawsuit once filed. Properly responding to the suit assures that your defenses to the debt will be considered by the judge before entering any court judgment. Also, filing a counterclaim presents your claim against the creditor/collector to assure that complete justice is achieved. If you don't timely assert these claims when the case is filed, the court will enter a judgment in favor of the creditor without your claim even being considered.

More than one-third[8] of all collection lawsuits filed may be defeated by simply responding to the Complaint[9]. Any response that asserts basic defenses will prevent any default judgment. In short, any answer to the Complaint (as long as the answer disputes at least one material allegation) is better than no response at all. Also, you should be mindful that if the collection case is meritless - which is true with 35% of all debt cases - the collector has pursued a barred claim, and the pursuit of such claim has violated the FDCPA, requiring an award of damages to the consumer.

The creditor or debt collector who files the collection lawsuit is named as the "Plaintiff." As with other types of civil lawsuits, the Plaintiff has the burden of proof with respect to its claims. This means that the Creditor must establish the existence of the

---

[8] According to a New York study, **35%** of debt cases filed in court are **completely meritless**. Legal Aid Society, NEDAP, MFY Legal Services, Urban Justice Center Community Development Project, *Debt Deception, How Debt Buyers Abuse the Legal System to Prey on Lower Income New Yorkers,* May 2010. Filing an Answer and asserting the appropriate defense would properly result in dismissal of the debt lawsuit in one out of three cases.

[9] Depending on the court where the lawsuit is filed, the initial document that sets forth the claims against the named defendant/debtor is called a "Complaint" or "Petition." Such document sets forth the claims that the plaintiff is making against the named defendants. Once a Complaint is served, there must be a timely filed Answer, or otherwise in the Court will deem all matters admitted and enter judgment against the Defendant.

debt, that the debtor ("Defendant") agreed to all terms by signing a contract, and that the debtor defaulted under required payment terms. All of the responsibility of establishing the contract and default is on the creditor. As a Defendant, the consumer <u>does not have the burden to prove anything</u>. The reality is that debt collectors and their attorneys rarely have sufficient information to meet this required burden of proof to the degree necessary to get a money judgment against a debtor. In order to prevail, the Plaintiff (collector) must produce signed copies of the original contract, proof of charges, advances or draws against such credit line, offsets and credits for payments made, and evidence of proper interest calculations that are supported by the original contract. If the creditor is lacking with respect to its documentation, it may not meet its required burden of proof, and the claim will be properly resolved in favor of the consumer. Courts are required to hold the Plaintiff to its burden of proof. The Plaintiff must prove its case in order for the court to enter a judgment. The one exception to the creditor having to prove its case is in the situation where the consumer defendant fails to file an Answer disputing the claims asserted. In such a situation, the Court is permitted to assume that all allegations are admitted by the consumer, and accordingly the Court will enter a default judgment.

Likewise, when the consumer asserts affirmative claims through counterclaim (i.e. consumer asserts right to recover damages for FCDPA, TILA violations or deceptive trade practices under state law), it is the consumer that has the burden of proof with respect to those counterclaims. With respect to claims for damages against the creditor, the consumer is acting as a "counter-plaintiff," and accordingly has the burden of proof to establish his or her claims in order to prevail with a judgment against the creditor/debt collector.

**Rule Number One:** **Always, Always, ALWAYS, file an Answer to the lawsuit!**

## WAYS TO GET EARLY NOTICE OF THE LAWSUIT

There are several ways to assure that you have early notice of a lawsuit that may be filed against you. Most courts have online docket systems that are searchable by the public. Normally, the debt collector only has only two choices of locations of courts to use for obtaining a judgment. The creditor generally must sue where the consumer resides (your home county and state); however, some states allow for suit to be filed "where the claim arose," or "where the contract forming the basis of litigation was executed." This means that a collector could sue you in the place where you lived at the time you incurred the debt as opposed to your home town. In the event the creditor decides to sue you in another state, there are procedures you may undertake to have the other state court dismiss the case, for a "lack of jurisdiction," or because the location of the court is inconvenient to you as a defendant. Unlike other situations, in the event you are sued in another state, it is extremely important to consult with an attorney in that other state, as local attorneys may not be able to advise you on the other state's laws. In most instances, the lawyer in the other state may file a motion to dismiss the case to cause the judge to dismiss the case, forcing the creditor to file again in your county of residence. Motions to Dismiss are usually considered "waived" by the court, unless such Motion is filed by the defendant as the first document in the case. If you fail to properly seek dismissal in an inconvenient location, you may be stuck with fighting the lawsuit in another state.

Most attorneys who file debt collection lawsuits will first send you their "30-day" letter on their law firm letterhead. Many attorneys will do so because their state law will not allow them to recover attorney fees unless they provide a thirty-day demand for settlement in advance of filing the lawsuit. Collection attorneys also provide this letter in attempt to comply with the FDCPA. This may be your final "heads-up" letter before being served with the lawsuit that a lawsuit is coming. Remember, the attorney who sends this letter before filing a lawsuit must comply with all provisions of the FDCPA, including advising you that his letter "is an attempt to collect a debt, and any information will be used for such purpose," and that you have the right to provide written notice within thirty days that you "dispute the validity of the debt," and the debt will be validated by sending you a verification documents through the mail. This 30-day letter should be your final wake-up call that it is time to gather all of your evidence to present their claim for violations of the Fair Debt Collection Practices Act and/or the provisions of law. This may also be your final opportunity to make an effective demand under the FDCPA, through a proper notice of claim and demand letter. This final thirty-day window is your opportunity to discourage the collector from moving forward in the courts to secure a judgment against you, your property, and your wages. Such is the time to give your final notice that you will be asserting claims for existing violations against the creditor/collector and the attorney.[10]

Assuming that the case is filed in the proper court, you are guaranteed to lose if you do not timely file an Answer to the Complaint. In filing an Answer to the Complaint, there are certain basic requirements which should not be ignored:

1. In the event the case is filed in a wrong court (improper venue), the Court must be alerted immediately through the Answer, Motion to Dismiss, or Motion to Transfer Venue filed separately. If you are challenging the location of the Court, you are better served to have an attorney assist you, as each state has different rules and procedures on what is required to challenge venue (location).

2. You must dispute each and every claim that you do not admit. Normally, this is done by admitting or denying paragraphs that are usually numbered in the Complaint. Sometimes you must state that you can neither admit nor deny an allegation, because you lack sufficient information after reasonable inquiry. Finally, you are ordinarily not penalized for denying a claim or paragraph, where you request to see proof. For example, it is not improper to deny the claim that you owe the creditor money, if you are not clear on whether or not you legally owe the specific dollar amount alleged. The bottom line: If you fail to deny any paragraph in the complaint, it is **deemed admitted**. Finally, you should generally

---

[10] See sample letter to collection attorney at Appendix C-3 at the end of this book.

deny all other claims that you have not expressly admitted. Include a statement at the end of your answer that says "Except as expressly admitted, the remaining allegations of the Complaint are denied." (A sample Answer to Complaint is located at Appendix C at the end of this book.)

3. You must raise AFFIRMATIVE DEFENSES. Courts are required to "liberally construe pleadings" to achieve "substantial justice." Therefore, you should not be penalized because you are not an attorney, or that your statements read differently from the way a lawyer might word the statements in the document. Affirmative defenses are specific reasons that you are stating you do not owe the claim. Affirmative defenses must be proven by you (the burden of proof shifts to the defendant), and it is essential for you to raise them through the filing of the Answer, if they apply. The following are examples of Affirmative Defenses:

a. **"Plaintiff's claims fail for lack of consideration."** (You are asserting that you did not get what was promised in exchange for your commitment to pay the debt).

b. **"Plaintiff's claims are barred by the applicable statute of limitations."** This means that the creditor waited too long to sue, and under applicable state law, the claim is barred.

c. **"Plaintiff has failed to satisfy all conditions precedent to recovery."** "Conditions precedent" is a legal term that simply means that the creditor was required to do other things before coming after you. This could be anything from providing a written demand to exercising rights against a cosigner, or seeking credit life or disability insurance benefits. Another example would be in the situation of secured loan, where the creditor repossessed collateral (such as a car), and thereafter has failed to sell the collateral in a commercially reasonable manner applying the proceeds to the debt, before suing the consumer.

d. **"Plaintiffs lending practices are in violation of (specific statutory provisions of law)"** (i.e. Truth in Lending Act Disclosures, authorized interest charges – Usury laws, as applicable; FDCPA; State Deceptive Trade Acts)

e. **"Plaintiff has <u>failed to state a claim</u> upon which relief may be granted."** Normally, this defense is urging to the judge that the lawsuit fails to adequately inform the basis of the lawsuit.

f. **"Plaintiff <u>lacks standing</u> to bring the claim."** Such a claim may be raised to force the collector to prove that such collector legally owns the debt. Remember, most collection lawsuits are brought by debt buyers who are not the original creditor. The company suing you will have to prove that it has a right to sue and recover from you. If the Plaintiff in the lawsuit is not the original creditor (Debt Buyer), the Debt Buyer may have to join all previous owners of the debt and the original creditor to the lawsuit. In these situations, Debt Buyers will likely walk away and dismiss the case. They are not in the collection game to spend money on lawyers and difficult procedures.

g. You may claim defenses by asserting that the creditor has failed to comply with statutory provisions of law, but you will likely have to be specific. For example, if you wish to claim that the creditor did not adequately disclose and explain requirements of the lending, you may need to reference the Federal Truth in Lending Act. My advice is that in asserting such defenses, to purposely be broad, by asserting something similar to the following: **"The transaction that forms the basis of litigation is unenforceable, as alleged, due to the fact that the Plaintiff has failed to make adequate disclosure of required information (interest calculations, default provisions, fees and costs of credit) in its lending documents, which cause the transaction to be in violation of state and federal law, including those requirements under the United States Federal Truth in Lending Act."**

**h. "Interest rates, charges and penalties applied to the transactions forming the basis of litigation are usurious and excessive, rendering the <u>contract unconscionable and unenforceable</u>."** (This is usually asserted where interest charged exceeds what is allowed by the law of your State.)

i. **The account has been "paid in part or in full."** (if applicable). This is referred to as the **<u>accord and satisfaction defense</u>.**

j. The debt has been discharged in bankruptcy. (if applicable).

k. The debt collector has violated the Fair Debt Collection Practices Act, entitling the consumer (Defendant) to actual and statutory damages. (This claim is usually raised by counterclaim, but it doesn't hurt to assert it as a defense.)

l. **The Defendant is "<u>not liable in the capacity that he/she has been sued</u>."** This defense is applicable when someone other than the defendant made the charges, or when the case is brought against the wrong person (a case of mistaken identity or identity theft). For example, if an individual is sued on a debt for his small business corporation, the corporation is liable for the debt, but the individual is not without a personal guarantee.

m. **Service of the Complaint was ineffective.** This is an important affirmative defense to raise in situations where the lawsuit was not served properly. Although the rules of court procedures differ in each state, all courts require that the lawsuit was served properly to assure due process of law. Some states, such as Colorado require documents to be filed with the court within ten days of service. If not, service is ineffective. Other courts require that Affidavits of Service be filed by the process server who delivered the court papers to the Defendant, demonstrating that delivery of litigation documents (Summons and Complaint) occurred within the required number of days after the lawsuit was filed. If you don't believe service was proper, you should assert the "insufficiency of process defense." Warning: Some states require an Affidavit or Sworn Answer (verified by notary under oath) to consider this defense. If it applies, get with an attorney in your state to assure it is asserted properly.

n. The claim is disputed as the creditor (Plaintiff) has included charges and fees not supported by the contract. (This is a FDCPA and Truth in Lending Act (TILA) violation.)

PRACTICE RULE: In most instances, you will never be penalized for raising the defense that you are unable to support with evidence at trial. The rule of practice should be to assert it, as long as you have a good faith basis to claim the defense. You have to remember that if you fail to raise a defense, it will be deemed waived, and you may not argue it later to the judge. If you are uncertain, raise the defense. The worst that can happen is that the judge finds against you on the defense, but nevertheless, by raising it, the Court will require the debt collector to prove that the defense does not apply. Always follow a rule of good faith. Do not make blatantly false statements to the Court, or there may be serious consequences.

## STATUTE OF LIMITATIONS DEFENSE

Studies have shown that 35% of collection lawsuits are entirely meritless. In a tremendous number of these cases, the creditor's debt claim is barred by the applicable Statute of Limitations. Every state imposes a deadline for a creditor or collector to file litigation in order to secure a judgment on a debt. The Statute of Limitations imposed upon creditors seeking a court judgment on their debts range from as little as **3 years**[11] to as much as **8+ years**[12]. The majority of other states have **4 to 6 year** statutes of limitations on debts arising from written contracts. In most instances, the statute of limitations is <u>measured from the date of default</u>. In other words, the question you should ask is how long has it been since I first went into default on the debt. If the default was more than the applicable statute of limitations period, the claim is barred and the creditor will not prevail in the litigation, <u>as long as you raise the affirmative defense that the</u>

---

[11] Alaska, Delaware, D.C., Maryland, New Hampshire, North Carolina and South Carolina all have three-year statute limitations for collection of debts, although the statutes vary.

[12] Louisiana, Illinois, Kentucky, Iowa, Wyoming, and West Virginia have statutes of limitations of 8 or more years.

debt is "barred by the applicable statute of limitations." Anyone in a situation of default with respect to a debt should be very careful, as creditors often will mislead the debtor prior to the filing of the lawsuit, and urge them to make a small payment. Some states consider that a new payment on a defaulted debt will renew the statute of limitations. If not careful, an effort to pay a debt that is in default may be used against you later, as the creditor may urge that your recent payment renewed the statute limitations for several more years. For example, Illinois law provides that the statute of limitations may be extended for an additional 10 years, upon a new payment being made, or a new promise to pay being accomplished.[13] You certainly do not want to begin paying on a debt that has been in default for many years, without fully understanding the statute of limitations. If the statute of limitations period has passed, the claim is barred as a matter of law. Any attempt to collect a barred debt is a violation of the Fair Debt Collection Practices Act (FDCPA). If a collector attempts to collect such a debt, it would be a tragedy for the consumer to make a new promise or payment which makes the debt collectible again, when the collector actually owes money to the debtor for violating the FDCPA.

At the time of publication, the statute limitations for the 50 states, as of January 2020, are as summarized here:

---

13 735 ILCS 5/13-206.

| State | Oral Contracts | Written Contracts | Promissory Notes | Open Accounts (Credit Cards) |
|---|---|---|---|---|
| Alabama | 6 | 6 | 6 | 3 |
| Alaska | 3 | 3 | 3 | 3 |
| Arizona | 3 | 6 | 6 | 3 |
| Arkansas | 3 | 5 | 3 | 3 |
| California | 2 | 4 | 4 | 4 |
| Colorado | 6 | 6 | 6 | 6 |
| Connecticut | 3 | 6 | 6 | 3 |
| Delaware | 3 | 3 | 3 | 4 |
| Florida | 4 | 5 | 5 | 4 |
| Georgia | 4 | 6 | 6 | 6 |
| Hawaii | 6 | 6 | 6 | 6 |
| Idaho | 4 | 5 | 5 | 5 |
| Illinois | 5 | 10 | 10 | 5 |
| Indiana | 6 | 6 | 10 | 6 |
| Iowa | 5 | 10 | 5 | 5 |
| Kansas | 3 | 5 | 5 | 3 |
| Kentucky | 5 | 10 | 15 | 5 |
| Louisiana | 10 | 10 | 10 | 3 |
| Maine | 6 | 6 | 6 | 6 |
| Maryland | 3 | 3 | 6 | 3 |
| Massachusetts | 6 | 6 | 6 | 6 |
| Michigan | 6 | 6 | 6 | 6 |
| Minnesota | 6 | 6 | 6 | 6 |
| Mississippi | 3 | 3 | 3 | 3 |
| Missouri | 5 | 10 | 10 | 5 |
| Montana | 5 | 8 | 8 | 5 |
| Nebraska | 4 | 5 | 5 | 4 |
| Nevada | 4 | 6 | 3 | 4 |

| State | Oral Contracts | Written Contracts | Promissory Notes | Open Accounts (Credit Cards) |
|---|---|---|---|---|
| New Hampshire | 3 | 3 | 6 | 3 |
| New Jersey | 6 | 6 | 6 | 6 |
| New Mexico | 4 | 6 | 6 | 4 |
| New York | 6 | 6 | 6 | 6 |
| North Carolina | 3 | 3 | 5 | 3 |
| North Dakota | 6 | 6 | 6 | 6 |
| Ohio | 6 | 8 | 15 | 6 |
| Oklahoma | 3 | 5 | 5 | 3 |
| Oregon | 6 | 6 | 6 | 6 |
| Pennsylvania | 4 | 4 | 4 | 4 |
| Rhode Island | 10 | 10 | 10 | 10 |
| South Carolina | 3 | 3 | 3 | 3 |
| South Dakota | 6 | 6 | 6 | 6 |
| Tennessee | 6 | 6 | 6 | 6 |
| Texas | 4 | 4 | 4 | 4 |
| Utah | 4 | 6 | 6 | 4 |
| Vermont | 6 | 6 | 5 | 3 |
| Virginia | 3 | 5 | 6 | 3 |
| Washington | 3 | 6 | 6 | 3 |
| West Virginia | 5 | 10 | 6 | 5 |
| Wisconsin | 6 | 6 | 10 | 6 |
| Wyoming | 8 | 10 | 10 | 8 |
| District of Columbia | 3 | 3 | 3 | 3 |

Note: <u>Laws change, so you must always check your state's Statutes at the time of being served with a lawsuit.</u>

Do not be overly discouraged if you happen to reside in a State that has a lengthy statute of limitations. Many states have a different statute of limitations for consumer credit card debt, or for revolving debts/debts on account. [For example, the State of Arizona, which has a six-year statute of limitations for contracts in writing, imposes a three-year statute of limitations for "open accounts."] Federal law essentially defines all credit cards as "open accounts." In considering the applicable Statute of Limitations for claims raised, you should confer with an attorney in your area. Most attorneys representing consumers will offer a free consultation and will quite often provide you information over the phone. You should review the applicable statute of limitations in your state with the attorney at the time of your first phone conference. Most attorneys handling debt relief in bankruptcy cases will provide a free consultation, or will answer this question over the phone without any cost to you.

Finally, if it is a "close call" situation, or you are not certain whether or not the claim is barred by the statute of limitations, you will not be penalized by raising the affirmative defense. Remember, as long as you have a "good faith" belief that the statute of limitations prevents the claim, you may assert the statute limitations defense. The judge deciding the case will have full knowledge of the law and determine whether or not the creditor's claim is time-barred.

## COUNTERCLAIMS

Most state laws require that if you are sued, and you have a claim against the person suing you, you are required to your claims in the same litigation. The Defendant's claim that the Plaintiff owes him money is referred to as a "Counterclaim." Courts will require that certain Counterclaims be asserted in the litigation, or otherwise they cannot be brought in a subsequent litigation. For example, if a painter who didn't get paid sues a homeowner for money he is owed, and the homeowner wishes to claim that the painter damaged the home while painting, the homeowner would be required to bring that counterclaim in the same case. Otherwise, the homeowner may not be able to file a separate lawsuit later. Counterclaims are "compulsory" (must be filed in same case) if the claim "arose from the same transaction or occurrence." Most courts hold the opinion that claims for violations by debt collectors under the Fair Debt Collection Practices Act are not so closely related to the contract and debt, so as to require that they must be asserted in the same collection lawsuit. In other words, if you do not countersue for your FDCPA claims in the collection case against you, you can still do so later. However, it doesn't hurt to assert these claims against the debt collector, if you have evidence of violations. Even though the state court judge may decide not to hear the Fair Debt Collection Practices Act claims, you have clearly alerted the creditor that you will be bringing them. FDCPA claims are generally required to be asserted in federal court and not the state courts. This is why state court judges will usually not hear the FDCPA violation case. Also, the judge deciding the debt case understands that the collection violations occurred at different times, such that they are not mandatory counterclaims to the creditor's lawsuit on the contract/debt. Do not be discouraged if the state court judge dismisses out the FDCPA counterclaims, as if that happens, it will be "without prejudice." Dismissing a case "without prejudice," means that the case may be reasserted in another court. Do however remember that you only have one year from the date of the FDCPA violation to file a Complaint for damages in federal court.

State judges also have the power to transfer the case to the federal court, if the Court feels that it your counterclaim asserting FDCPA violations raises an issue that may only be heard by the federal court (exclusive jurisdiction in the federal court). Most often, transfers to the federal court occurs as a result of a request by the collection attorney, through the filing of a Notice of Removal. A Notice of Removal transfers the entire case over to the federal court in the same district. Likewise, you can file a Notice of Removal of the case to have the case transferred in the federal court. There are specific procedures to remove a case to federal court that you will have to follow if removing the case.

Provided that the case is supported by evidence, it is always advisable to file the Counterclaim alleging violation of the Federal Debt Collection Practices Act (FDCPA) and/or the Truth in Lending Act (TILA) at the same time as answering the lawsuit. Even if the case is removed to the federal court, you have filed the case within the applicable statute of limitations. Remember, you can only complain of FDCPA violations occurring within one year before you raise them by filing the appropriate documents in Court. When you make a Counterclaim, remember you must allege that you were damaged, and that you are asking the Court for affirmative relief in the form of an award of "all actual, incidental and consequential damages, statutory damages under available at law and equity (FDCPA, TIL, and State law) in additional to an award of all costs and attorney fees incurred." A sample Counterclaim is provided at Appendix C "The War Chest" at the end of this book.

## IMPLEADING THIRD PARTIES

Some state courts permit impleading of other third parties. For example if a person is sued, and her former husband is obligated to pay the debt by virtue of a divorce decree, she would have the right (depending on the court) to request that the court implead the former husband into the case as an additional defendant. If an employee incurred a debt at the request of her former employer, likewise, certain courts would permit the employee to implead the former employer as an additional defendant. Unfortunately, the fact that someone else may have directed the transaction usually will not act as a complete defense. Usually, the employee and the former wife in the above example would be held liable anyway. But if the court entered a judgment against these other individuals, the creditor might collect its claim completely from them, providing some protection to the person who innocently entered into the transaction.

## HOW TO DEFEAT THE CREDITOR WHO ALREADY HAS A COURT JUDGMENT

Once the creditor has a court judgment it becomes very difficult to avoid the creditor. It is often too late to go to a judge and argue that you have a defense to the debt. However, if you were unaware that the civil case was ever filed against you, until the collector contacts you and tells you "we have a judgment against you," you may have some appellate rights. Every state has different rules on challenging a judgment. For this reason, I will not detail procedures here. This is an area which would prompt you to contact a local attorney, to understand what rights you have to challenge a Judgment. States vary with respect to their timetables on permitting a person to come into court and challenge judgments. Normally, there is a specified period of time which can range anywhere from six months, or expand up to ten years. Most states require that you file something in the same court that issued the judgment and request that the judgment to be vacated. The most common ground asserted for vacating a judgment is "insufficiency of process." ("I was never served!") If this is the case, you may be successful in getting the State Court to vacate the judgment; however, once you successfully get the judgment removed, the judge may then set the matter for trial, and if you don't have a defense, you have not accomplished much more than rolling back the case to an earlier phase, forcing you to defend the claim. If there is no valid defense, you may find yourself in for the same result after a trial.

# The Creditor That Has a Judgment Is Liable for Any Violation of the FDCPA

Although the debt collector with a judgment has everything it needs to begin levying on your assets and wages, it continues to be governed by the Fair Debt Collection Practices Act. If the collector begins making phone calls and sending letters, is required to provide all notices and disclosures under the FDCPA. Also remember, that if the debt is now owned by a Debt Buyer, that the Debt Buyer is also governed by the FDCPA. Efforts to collect the judgment – contacting employers, sending letters, threats by attorneys, all may be in violation of the FDCPA. In short, FDCPA violations may continue to occur after you have lost the civil lawsuit. The collector and/or debt buyer will continue to undertake effort to collect money from you, and will quite often blatantly violate what is required under the law.

Even if the debt buyer or collector already has a judgment against you, their efforts may be defeated through proper documentation on your part of FDCPA violations. Once you have evidence of these violations, as mentioned before, the collector is strictly liable and owes you damages. Most often, if you owe them money, and they owe you money, the matter can be resolved with an "everybody walk away and take nothing" result. Documenting these violations and asserting your rights is critical to defeating the debt buyer/collector who violates federal law. Even though a court judgment has already been obtained by the creditor/collector, it may be defeated in the face of your asserting your rights under federal and state laws.

# Chapter 9

## PROTECTING YOUR ASSETS

"The personal right to acquire property, which is a natural right, gives to property, when acquired, a right to protection, as a social right." James Madison

Once a creditor has presented its claim by the filing of a lawsuit in a court of competent jurisdiction, the creditor is in a position where it is extraordinarily close to having the ability to seize assets and garnish bank accounts and wages. In the United States, our Constitution guarantees that no person may be deprived of life, liberty, or property, without due process of law. Courts have essentially construed this constitutional protection as applying to civil cases - that the person sued for money damages has a right to defend the case. This right to oppose the allegations of the creditor and present evidence is the only "due process" afforded. Once the creditor secures a court judgment, that creditor will have the power under the law of the consumer's State to begin seizing assets.

If the consumer is well-familiar with basic asset protection laws, and if proper planning has been undertaken, money and assets can be protected from the reach of the judgment creditor. State laws and the federal bankruptcy laws give the power of creditors to undo and set aside transfers of property occurring last minute. Accordingly, it is essential that if a person may end up defaulting on his debts, that asset protection plans and procedures be considered early in the game.

Because of the right of citizens not to be deprived of property without due process of law, creditors generally must get a court judgment before they can seize property. Certain creditors can reach assets without a court judgment, such as the IRS or state child-support agency that holds a child support lien. Additionally, a secured creditor, such as a mortgage lender or vehicle lender, may have a right of repossession or foreclosure, which affords the secured creditor the right to take specific property (collateral) in the event of a default under the loan, without first going to court. Unsecured creditors (such as credit card lenders, medical account holders, or other entities holding general unsecured claims) may not seize property without first getting a judgment in a court of law. As the law requires that general creditors prevail in court before having the power to seize assets, consumers are afforded the time and opportunity to plan to protect assets, if they do not delay. Once a judgment is procured, there is little to no time to do anything to protect assets.

## Understand the Exemption Laws of Your State

Every state in the United States has a set of personal property exemptions. Property exemptions consist of a list of property that each person has a right to own and maintain, which is free from execution (seizure) by general creditors. Assets that are outside of these prescribed exemptions are subject to seizure by creditors, and are assets which can be lost in bankruptcy proceedings.

As this publication concerns defeating your creditors through utilizing procedures and legal processes, only a basic overview of asset protection will be attempted. For a detailed analysis of property protections and comprehensive review of asset protection techniques, read *The Asset Protection Playbook* available through *Legal Playbooks®*. Such separate publication details protections of personal assets, as well as business assets through formation and structure of Limited Liability Companies (LLCs). For purposes of this book, only general concepts of asset protection are covered.

The first step in assuring that you do not lose valuable property to your creditors is to focus on the areas of protection which provide the highest dollar amounts of protection. Generally, no matter where you live, these will be the protections afforded as to homestead and retirement benefits.

## Homestead Protection

Essentially every state, with the exception of New Jersey, provides for homestead protection. States vary in how they interpret whether or not specific property can be protected as a home. For example, in the state of Arizona, you must actually reside in the homestead, but the homestead can be virtually anything used as a dwelling. In Arizona, a homestead may include a travel trailer or recreational vehicle, as long as the debtor uses it as a home. In some states, such as Texas, a homestead may only be claimed upon land and improvements. Texas lawyers often explain to their clients that if their mobile home is on wheels, it is not protected; if it is on blocks, it is not. The first step in understanding homestead is to assure that property that you may acquire and want to protect qualifies under the homestead statute of your state.

Homestead protections are also generally limited as to value, with only a few exceptions (Texas and Florida). In determining whether or not the homestead is within the value established by a particular state, the focus is on the equity, and not the gross market value of the property. For example, in a state such as Arizona (which has a $400,000.00 homestead limit), a person can own a home worth $600,000.00, and if that person has mortgages on the property that exceed the sum of $200,000.00, then the home is protected, as the equity is less than the $400,000.00 cap. Other states, such as Texas and Florida, have homestead protections that are limited only by acreage, and not by value. In these states, the home is protected, irrespective of the value of the home. In Texas, the acreage limitation for a family is up to 10 acres in an urban area, and up to 200 acres in a rural area (100 acres for rural homestead, if not married). Generally, most states permit only one homestead protection and will not permit a second homestead protection for the spouse. Beware: The dollar value of the protection may be affected if the person hits bankruptcy, in situations where he or she only recently acquired the homestead.

## Retirement Accounts

Most states and the federal government provide that retirement accounts are protected from the reach of creditors. The policy in protecting such accounts is that the government has an interest in retirees being able to provide for their own support during years when they are unable to work. States vary with respect to their laws as to how much money may be protected in a retirement account. The federal government provides 100% protection with respect to certain ERISA-based plans. Many States likewise provide 100% protection of most retirement benefits, provided that the money that was put into retirement satisfied requirements of law (contribution rules). If a person suddenly dumps $100,000.00 into an IRA, the great majority of such funds would not be protected, as the IRA maximum limits on annual contributions have been exceeded. However, if a person is in the first quarter of the year, and he did not make a contribution for a previous year, he may be able to contribute for both last year and this year, as long as the contribution is made before April 15. This would enable a married couple to make a lawful contribution of $22,000.00 to $26,000.00 ($6,000.00 per spouse, per year -- $7,000.00 if age 50 or older – 2020 IRA annual limits) between January and April 15, which would protect this amount of proceeds from the reach of creditors. There are rules that provide that certain contributions may be set aside if a bankruptcy case is filed within a specified period of time after the contribution (i.e. Arizona provides that contributions made within 120 days prior to bankruptcy may be set aside).

# Section 529 College Education Plans

A Section 529 College Education Plan is an education savings plan that is operated by a state or educational institution for purposes of helping families set aside funds for future education costs. The name arises from Section 529 of the Internal Revenue Code. Such plans may be used to save money for college for dependents, and quite often provide benefits of tax deductions and locking educational costs at today's dollars as opposed to the future cost of education. Most importantly, Section 529 plans may not be invaded by general creditors under the laws of at least twenty-five states and under federal bankruptcy law. As with retirement contributions, there are limits on the amount that may be contributed. However, a person can invest significant amounts, being that the contribution limits are based upon "per child," and because Section 529 permits contribution of significant amounts for present and future years. One benefit to contributing to a Section 529 Plan is that the funds may be later withdrawn from the plan, if needed, with applicable taxes and penalties assessed. In the event a person hits bankruptcy, contributions made to 529 Plans within one year prior to bankruptcy are not protected. Only $5,000.00 of contributions per beneficiary are protected if the contribution was made between one and two years prior to bankruptcy.

## Personal Property Assets

Each state has a schedule of personal property assets that are protected. Such protections generally include household goods, furnishings, clothing and jewelry, within certain limits. Exemptions also include a protection for a vehicle, but equity limits vary. For example, Washington only protects $6,500.00 of equity in two vehicles for a married couple, where Texas allows any value as long as the aggregate value of all personal property (including vehicles) does not exceed the limit of $100,000.00 for a married couple. States vary on how many vehicles are protected (i.e. Texas protects one vehicle per member of the household who holds a driver's license). Most states provide very little or no protection for cash or money in bank accounts. Social Security Act benefits are protected under federal law. Workers' compensation benefits are generally protected in most states. Wages are not fully protected in the great majority of states. In those states, creditors with judgments may garnish a percentage of each paycheck. A few states – North Carolina, Pennsylvania, and South Carolina - do not allow garnishments to certain types of creditors (i.e. credit cards or "commercial" debts). Texas does not allow garnishment of wages to any creditor, other than for unpaid child support. Federal law (Consumer Credit Protection Act) provides some protection as to garnishment, permitting no more than 25% of disposable income to be garnished.

## PROTECTION OF BUSINESS ASSETS

Many states now provide asset protection to certain types of businesses. Limited Liability Companies (LLCs) with more than one Member (owner) are provided protection under what is now becoming the majority view in most states. State legislatures realize that if partners jointly own a business, one partner who has personal debt problems could cause the entire business to be wiped out. If one partner has judgments against him, the judgment creditor could begin seizing partnership assets. This would result in loss of business assets to the other partners, who were not liable for the sued partner's debts. Many states have passed Statutes that are designed to address this problem. In such states, a creditor that takes a judgment against a person who owns a membership interest in a Limited Liability Company may only receive distributions due to the Member (judgment debtor) under a Charging Order. A Charging Order only requires that the LLC make payment of dividend distributions, if any, to the creditor.

A Charging Order state will not permit the creditor to seize and dispose of the business assets. A discussion of protecting business assets through properly organized LLCs is the subject matter of *The Asset Protection Playbook,* a *Legal Playbooks*® publication.

## BANKRUPTCY REFORM LEGISLATION

In recent years, Congress and the federal courts have undertaken to reform bankruptcy protections and procedures. Additionally, state legislatures have also undertaken to reform some of the property protections and remedies available to creditors. Most of the changes in the law relate to situations where money or assets are transferred, or transmuted into other types of property, close in time prior to bankruptcy. If money or property is transferred with the intent to hinder, delay, or otherwise to thwart the creditor, in situations where a debtor is insolvent (unable to pay his debts, or found to be liable upon court judgments) such transfers will often set aside. Assets that would not otherwise be able to be reached by the creditor can be now sold to recover funds for creditors, as result of the debtor's last-minute activities to transfer or dispose of the assets. The only sure way to understand whether or not attempts to protect assets will result in the protection sought is to confer with a qualified attorney who understands the rules and principles of law.

Generally, if a person is concerned about the ability to timely meet their obligations and pay their debts, a basic level of attention and focus should be directed in maintaining protected assets. I have had many encounters with people overwhelmed with debt who did knee-jerk things to avoid their creditors. It makes no sense to cash out an asset that is protected, or to transfer a protected asset to someone else. A homestead protection may be lost if the home is transferred into another person's name. Likewise, if the person is in trouble, and needs to sell off assets to pay creditors, it only makes sense that the person should focus on selling those assets that have no protection.

If a person is a small business owner, or engages in a profession that has some degree of risk of being sued, it makes good sense to put your hard-earned money into protected assets. By the time there is a threat of a pending lawsuit, it may be too late to sell off assets and move money into protected places. Likewise, transferring assets in the face of credit problems can result in the creditor successfully getting the court to set aside such transfers in order to bring money back to be paid upon the creditor's claim. Asset protection planning must take place at a time well in advance of any problems with creditors. Just as it makes sense to buy insurance to protect from unforeseen disasters, it makes sense to prepare to protect your estate. Hopefully, there will never be a situation where assets are being sought by creditors. However, if the unpredictable adversity arises, proper planning will provide you and your family necessary protection.

# Chapter 10

## THE ULTIMATE WEAPON BANKRUPTCY

"At the end of every seven years you shall grant a release of debts. And this is the form of the release: Every creditor who has lent anything to his neighbor shall release it." *Holy Bible, Book of Deuteronomy, Chapter 15, Verse 1 (KJV).*

Most people are aware that federal law permits relief from creditors, through filing of a Petition in Bankruptcy. Bankruptcy generally will afford relief in the form of a court-ordered "Discharge," which eliminates all debts that are dischargeable under the law. Certain debts may survive bankruptcy, such as child support obligations, criminal fines, certain taxes and student loans. Also, if the court decides that the debt arose as a product of fraud or dishonesty the debt may survive a Bankruptcy Discharge. Bankruptcy provides the most certain relief from creditors, as a fresh start is essentially guaranteed. Yes, <u>guaranteed</u>! After twenty-one years of practice, I have found that this is one area of law where I can guarantee my client will receive the relief, as long as two important things happen: (1) My client must be completely honest and make all disclosures as required by law; (2) my client must participate in all required meetings and required court hearings. As long as the debtor follows through with his or her responsibilities, and the case is handled by a competent attorney, a bankruptcy discharge is absolute and certain, allowing the debtor to emerge debt-free. What is not guaranteed in a bankruptcy case is the degree that the debtor may sustain loss of assets or sustain an adverse impact to his future monthly income. For this reason, it is most critical that the debtor employ a competent bankruptcy attorney, who has experience and knowledge in bankruptcy law and procedures.

Although I will highlight basic bankruptcy principles, my goal in this chapter is to not to provide a lecture as to bankruptcy laws and procedures, but rather to educate as to how to protect from loss of income and assets in the bankruptcy process. Just as it is entirely ethical and legal to plan with respect to reducing income taxes, it is entirely ethical and legal to plan in advance of bankruptcy to minimize loss of money or property.

Hiring a qualified attorney to handle a bankruptcy case is about the least expensive matter one could hire an attorney to do. In fact, paying an attorney to handle an entire bankruptcy case usually costs less than hiring an attorney to defend even one single debt lawsuit. It perplexes me as to why people will allow themselves to be misled that they should file their bankruptcy case without a lawyer. Over the past two decades we have seen companies begin to advertise that "You don't need a lawyer!" and that you should hire a "petition preparer" or "paralegal" to handle the matter. The truth of the matter is that these individuals are charging a fee (often more than attorneys charge) to fill out the federal forms in the case (all of which are available for free on the internet). These non-attorneys are not permitted to give any legal advice as they are not competent to do so; however, they routinely break the law and give advice in the process of typing up forms. Additionally, these non-lawyers are not permitted to attend and participate in hearings or court proceedings. Sadly, a great number of these non-attorneys are disbarred lawyers or paralegals who were fired for misconduct in their prior legal job for not following correct procedures. As with any professional relationship, you should do some basic research about the attorney you hire to handle your bankruptcy case. Believe it or not, the least experienced and least qualified attorneys often charge more money than experienced bankruptcy attorneys with years of experience.

I often say that if you want to change your name or fight a simple traffic ticket, you probably can get the job done without a lawyer. However, with a bankruptcy case filing, you are stuck with the results, good or bad. If a bankruptcy trustee is going to seize and sell an asset, you may not be able to stop him. You may find that the asset could have been saved, but that you did not claim the proper legal exemption (protection). If a creditor is not properly listed in the bankruptcy, or the wrong address is provided, such error could result in the debt not being discharged in the bankruptcy. If information is omitted that is required to be disclosed, the discharge can be denied by the court, which not only means that the debt survives bankruptcy, but also means that the debt may **never be discharged in another bankruptcy case in the future**. Finally, if something goes wrong in the case, and you just want out of the whole process, you may not be able to dismiss the case in the face of an objection by a creditor or your bankruptcy trustee.

There are situations where people cannot afford a lawyer, no matter how low the lawyer's fee may be. Situations like this usually involve people who have very little in the way of income and assets. I recommend to these people that if you are going to represent yourself in a bankruptcy case without an attorney, at least be sure you undertake a few protective measures before filing the bankruptcy case. These simple procedures cost nothing, and are the next best thing for the person who cannot afford any attorney.

## Schedule a Free Consultation With a Competent Attorney

No matter where you live in the United States, a free consultation with a bankruptcy lawyer is available to you. The reality is that there are just too many lawyers. In order for lawyers to get your business, they must convince you of their grasp and understanding of your legal problem. Additionally, most attorneys are unable to communicate a precise attorney fee without understanding the complexity of the issues involved. This means that the attorney must analyze the legal issues, and determine which course of action is best to be undertaken. Will the client need a Chapter 7 or Chapter 13? Should bankruptcy be considered at all? Because legal decisions cannot be properly recommended without the attorney having a complete clear understanding of relevant information, a competent attorney will always offer a "free consultation." Avoid attorneys who charge a "consultation fee." There is a reason why they charge this fee. It is usually because their fees are so much higher than other attorneys, that they do not get hired very often. Attorneys who offer "free consultations," understand that their time is valuable, and that they will make no money unless their fees are reasonable and competitive with other attorneys.

It is extremely important that your free consultation be meaningful, and that the conference be held with an attorney qualified to render appropriate advice. Just as with other important decisions, be careful not to be drawn in by advertising. There is a reason why some lawyers buy up billboards and run TV commercials. I don't mean to offend the big advertising attorneys, but you must ask yourself "Why do they spend so much money on advertising? Will I pay a higher fee if I hire this attorney to fund his advertising budget?" Sadly, we live in the age where consumers are bombarded with so much advertising that it is very difficult to determine the level of competence of the attorney from reviewing their ads. With the emergence of Internet advertising, even the least qualified and least skilled attorneys may run an Internet advertisement that appears far up the screen ahead of other very skilled attorneys. In the past, it was not as difficult to seek out an attorney, as most attorneys placed yellow page ads that described their experience and expertise. In the modern day of the Internet, lawyer's advertisements are usually created and driven by non-attorney advertising companies, doing their best to draw you in to the least qualified attorneys. You may not even see the experienced attorney on the Internet, or otherwise, you have to make your way through twenty pages of web pages or more to find the needle in the haystack.

I always recommend in seeking out an attorney that you find one that is "Board Certified" in a field that demonstrates the attorney's special level of competence in the type of cases he or she handles. This information can be gathered through professional certifying organizations, such as the American Board of Certification (national certification board), or the local State Bar Association, who certifies attorneys within the State having specialty knowledge and practice. In order for an attorney to become Board Certified, the attorney must demonstrate special expert knowledge and competence in the area of law in which the attorney seeks to be certified. The attorney must pass a comprehensive exam. Other lawyers in the community must recommend the attorney as being one known to have demonstrated special knowledge and ability in the field of practice. Some of the recommending attorneys must have been attorneys who have fought the attorney on the other side of legal cases. The lawyer must be in good standing in all states where the lawyer is admitted to practice. Most Board Certified attorneys do not charge more than non-certified attorneys.

You should be able to tell by your first meeting whether or not you have received a competent free consultation. Avoid any law firm that sends a non-lawyer in the room instead of an attorney. Don't be afraid to ask right up front "Are you an attorney?" Also, don't be afraid to ask an attorney "How long have you been practicing? How much experience do you have with bankruptcy cases?" You should be able to notice immediately by the attorney's reaction, whether or not the attorney is competent. Competent attorneys pride themselves on their experience, ability and reputation. Also, if the first subject of the conversation relates to fees, you know you were in the wrong place. I remember in my early days of practice, my father, who was an attorney in North Texas, gave me an old sign that had been hand-painted, which had hung outside of the door of a law firm back in the 1930s. The old sign said "Attorney's Office – Consultations 25 Cents – Your Lawyer is Your Friend" The old sign was displayed in the lobby of my first law firm, and earned many comments and complements. The best lawyer to review your legal problem is one who truly cares. There are many lawyers who treat the practice of law as an admirable profession. They awake each morning with a desire to help people in need. They get excited when they recognize a legal problem, and understand how to solve the matter to the client's benefit. I learned from an early mentor in law practice that if you care about your clients -- truly care -- you will never have any problem getting business. My father, who was a prominent well known attorney in Texas, would always run to the phone to speak to any person who called, even if their legal matter was not one he was interested in handling. After he would get off the phone, he would explain that, although he knew before he got on the phone that there was no legal case to be handled for the client, he would always speak to anyone who needed help. He would say, "Even though that person does not have a case, I now have a client for life."

Through meaningful consultation, you should get a general idea of the type of bankruptcy case that should be filed. Lawyers do have families to feed, and sometimes it is best not to tell the attorney that you have no intent and employing his or her services. Many times, through such consultations, after revealing the value of legal services and how to accomplish excellent results, the client would make a decision to hire, where they thought they would not hire before coming into the office.

Some state and local Bar Associations have lawyer referral services, whereby local attorneys agree to give at least one-half hour consultation to anyone who calls the referral services phone number, for a nominal fee (usually $20.00). One problem with these Referral Services is that you may not be directed to an attorney who is most competent to review bankruptcy issues with you. Bankruptcy law is a very specialized area of law, so you must be sure that you meet with an attorney who handles bankruptcy cases, and not just an attorney who holds a general law license without knowledge of bankruptcy law. Referral services will refer indiscriminately to all attorneys who are on the list, without regard to whether or not the attorney is competent to handle any specific type of legal matter. Usually, you are better off finding the bankruptcy specialist who will offer the free consultation.

## The Meeting

In meeting with a competent attorney, it is important that you make full disclosure of your assets, income, and debts. You can only receive a meaningful consultation if you disclose such important matters. When you confer with an attorney, your communications are privileged. If you have questions about the confidentiality of your discussions, you should ask the attorney at the beginning of your meeting. Normally, you do not need to bring documentation with you, as a competent attorney will have you fill out a short questionnaire, and will ask the right questions necessary to recommend a Chapter of Bankruptcy.

# The Law of Bankruptcy

> Congress is authorized to "enact uniform Laws on the subject of Bankruptcies throughout the United States." *United States Constitution* (Article 1, Section 8, Clause 4, commonly known as "The Bankruptcy Clause.)"

Bankruptcy law is part of our United States Constitution. Bankruptcy laws exist thanks to our founding fathers, who assured that all people in the United States would be entitled to relief of bankruptcy. The founding fathers, and their ancestors, were among those who fled European nations to escape certain "evils of the crown." One of these evils was the fact that these tyrannical nations operated debtor's prisons. In these nations, if a person could not pay his debts, the presiding tribunal would issue an order that the person be jailed and confined, until a family member or other person paid off the debts, after which the debtor would be released from prison. In these societies, wealthy landowners would offer to pay off a prisoner's debts, in exchange for a contract for that prisoner to work for the paying party for the rest of their life. Such resulted in people being purchased out of debtor's prison as slaves. In these foreign nations, a contract was a contract, and the law was unwavering, even if the contract denied the person of essential freedoms and liberties. Prisoners were forced to make the hard decision of "Do I want to stay in prison the rest of my life?" or "Do I want to leave prison and work as an involuntary servant for the wealthy landowners, in exchange for basic food and provisions?" Out of love, family members of debtors in prison would contract away their lives, in order to free the imprisoned family member. Our forefathers, in drafting the document that defined basic freedoms and guarantees to all citizens, included the right of bankruptcy protection and a guaranteed financial fresh start. The United States Constitution empowered Congress to create a bankruptcy law system, which Congress has done through the United States Bankruptcy Code.

# A Fresh Start
# Chapter 7 Bankruptcy
## (A Basic Overview)

Chapter 7 of the Bankruptcy Code is a bankruptcy case in which the debtor does not make any scheduled monthly payments to its creditors. Chapter 7 rules do not require that the debtor use any future income to pay his creditors. Rather, Chapter 7 provides a complete discharge without payment of any kind. As a result of changes in Bankruptcy Law which took effect October 17, 2005, only the lower half of income earners in the United States may file under Chapter 7. Individuals who are in the top half of income earners are generally only eligible to file under Chapter 11 or Chapter 13, which are chapters that require ongoing plan payments to creditors. These rules vary depending on the type of debts (i.e. business vs. consumer debt).

In order to determine whether an individual qualifies for Chapter 7, a look-back of all earnings received within the six months prior to filing of the bankruptcy case must occur. For a wage earner, six months of gross earnings must be computed, and then annualized over twelve months to determine annualized gross income. The determination of whether or not a person is in the upper or lower half of income earners is made by comparing the individual to all other individuals in their county, as reported on income tax returns. This comparison is known as the "Means Test." The "means test" also considers the size of the household of the bankruptcy filer. If the bankruptcy filer is married with two children, then his household income is compared with all families of four in the county of residence. In determining whether or not the person is eligible for Chapter 7, it is important to understand the "means test" numbers. These numbers are revised and published by the Federal Government every six months. By way of example, as of November 1, 2024, an individual or couple with consumer debt considering filing under Chapter 7 must establish that their gross household income is below the following "means test" numbers, depending on the size of the household:

MEANS TEST (Phoenix, Maricopa County AZ)

| Family Size | Gross Income Annually | Monthly |
|---|---|---|
| 1 | $ 68,887.00 | $ 5,741.00 |
| 2 | $ 83,027.00 | $ 6.919.00 |
| 3 | $ 99,961.00 | $ 8,330.00 |
| 4 | $ 110,040.00 | $ 9,170.00 |
| 5 | $ 119,940.00 | $ 9,995.00 |
| 6 | $ 129,840.00 | $ 10,820.00 |
| 7+ | $9.900.00 for each additional dependent | |

Mean tests numbers for each county in the United States, and means test calculators, are available online to determine whether or not a person qualifies for Chapter 7. It is not as simple as it may seem. A wage earner may receive three paychecks and one month, and two pay checks in the next. A person may be over the allowed number, but drop below the number if there are more recent paychecks with less income. A person may be above the applicable mean income, but have certain other obligations (monthly debts) that may bring the number down enough to qualify the person for a Chapter 7 filing. If debts are principally business debts, the means test may not apply at all. A qualified attorney can determine whether or not the person is eligible for Chapter 7, by gathering basic financial information such as tax returns and pay stubs.

# The Downside to Filing Chapter 7

The downside to filing a Chapter 7 case, for some people, is that Chapter 7 is the Chapter of bankruptcy where people can lose property. Since you are not required to make a monthly plan payment in the future (as with a Chapter 13 case), you have agreed, by filing the Chapter 7, that to the extent you own any property over and above what your state may allow you to keep, such (nonexempt) property may be taken by a trustee liquidator and sold to bring money to your creditors. Each state has a different set of property protections which also apply in bankruptcy. States widely differ in what property of its citizens is protected and what property is not protected. For example, the states of Texas and Florida have homestead protections that are limited only in acreage, but which are not limited in value. A married couple owning a Texas ranch with five houses worth ten million dollars can file bankruptcy, and not lose the homestead ranch, as long as the ranch is on less than 200 acres. On the other extreme, the state of New Jersey provides no homestead protection at all to its citizens. Some states offer as little $5,000.00 for homestead protection. Other states are in the middle, placing dollar limits on the value of equity in the homestead. In these states, if the equity in the home exceeds the allowed homestead amount, the home can be sold, with the exemption amount going to the debtor, and any amount above the exemption limit going to the creditors.

Some states will allow a debtor filing a bankruptcy case to utilize what the federal Congress has declared should be the minimum protections for debtors in bankruptcy. These are known as the "Federal Exemptions." Although Congress drafted these, Congress gave the states the power to prevent their citizens from using these protections in bankruptcy cases. Some states allow the claiming of federal exceptions in bankruptcy, and some force their citizens to claim only those property exemptions provided under the state's law.

When a Chapter 7 case is filed, each case is assigned to a Chapter 7 Trustee. These Trustees are paid a small amount of money per case, but they also are permitted to keep a percentage (as high as 25%) of any money that the Trustee may recover for creditors. This is where Chapter 7 Trustees make their real money. Like many people on commission, the more money they find, the more money they make. As you might imagine, Chapter 7 Trustees are usually very good at finding money. The United States Justice Department gives these Trustees access to information such as nationwide motor vehicle division records, and other databases that may show ownership or transfer of assets.

All documents that are signed by a debtor in bankruptcy are signed under penalties of perjury. The law imposes very serious fines and penalties for any dishonest person filing bankruptcy.

Just as with income tax returns, when bankruptcy documents are signed, the person signing must swear under oath that the statements are true, accurate and complete, acknowledging his or her understanding of the fines and penalties for false or misleading statement. Bankruptcy filers are advised that there may be *up to a $500,000.00 fine or five (5) years imprisonment (or both)* for any "material misstatement or omission" in their bankruptcy documents. If a person accidentally forgets or overlooks to disclose a material asset, that person can be prosecuted for bankruptcy fraud. Additionally, the Bankruptcy Court has the power to deny the bankruptcy discharge, which applies to the present bankruptcy, as well as any bankruptcy case in the future.

## The Power of the Chapter 7 Trustee

Once a Chapter 7 bankruptcy case is filed, the appointed Chapter 7 Trustee immediately becomes the owner of all property of the debtor that is not specifically exempted under applicable law. By way of example, if a person owns a home and a rental property, although the home may be protected as homestead, the rental property immediately becomes property owned by the Chapter 7 Trustee. This Trustee has the power to sell the non-exempt assets to recover money for creditors. However, the Trustee does not have the power to take away protected exempt property. Sometimes, a Chapter 7 trustee will decide that it is not worth his time and effort to sell a nonexempt asset. For example, if a bankruptcy debtor owns an old boat with little value, and the engine is not running, although the Trustee has the power to sell the asset, he may decide to abandon his interest in the boat, and at the end of the bankruptcy case, the boat is retained by the debtor.

In order for the Chapter 7 Trustee to determine whether or not there are assets that may be sold, the Trustee will look over Bankruptcy documents, and conduct an interview of the debtor, usually held in the United States Bankruptcy Court building in the district where the case is pending. Creditors will receive notice of this meeting and are invited to attend and ask questions. Rarely, do creditors or their attorneys attend the face-to-face meeting (Section 341 Meeting of Creditors). Most creditors understand that the assigned Chapter 7 Trustee will diligently review the case, asking appropriate questions, and that in the event assets are taken and sold, that a distribution of funds will be made to creditors. However, there are occasions when a creditor will hire an attorney to show up for this one required meeting that every person filing bankruptcy must attend.

A very important additional power of a Chapter 7 Trustee is the power to set aside transfers of property made prior to bankruptcy. When a bankruptcy case is filed, the debtor must answer a number of questions known as the "Statements of Financial Affairs." These questions ask about transactions that may have occurred within specified periods of time prior to the filing of the bankruptcy case. For example, a bankruptcy debtor is required to list all property transferred to any person within two years prior to the filing of the bankruptcy case. In the event that a debtor transferred his interest in a boat to his brother or sister prior to bankruptcy, such would have to be disclosed. Transfers to anyone in advance of bankruptcy, without that person paying fair value for the property transferred, will result in a fraudulent transfer action being filed by the trustee against the third party. In short, Chapter 7 Trustees will investigate, and chase down any money or property that the debtor transferred away to someone else prior to bankruptcy. Even innocent transactions can be set aside. For example, when a bankruptcy case is filed, the debtor must disclose any payments made to a relative or family member within one year prior to the bankruptcy. This would include repayment of any legitimate debt. If the debtor discloses that her mother helped her pay her moving expenses last year, and when the debtor received her tax refund, she paid back her mother, this payment would be set aside. Normally with respect to payment of debts prior to bankruptcy, the Trustee can chase down and bring back any payment made within 90 days to an *ordinary* creditor, but go back as far as one year with respect to any payments to insiders *(relatives or business partners)*. The idea of setting aside preferential payments is that a fair distribution should occur. It's not that the debtor did anything wrong by paying back Mom, or paying a creditor right before bankruptcy, but rather, that it is simply not fair that one creditor got paid in full, while others got paid nothing. When a Trustee seeks to set aside a preferential transfer, normally it will not harm the bankruptcy debtor, but it impacts the third-party, who may be a relative or someone who matters. When the money comes back, the Trustee gets a percentage as a commission.

Rules on Preferential Payments

- A Trustee may set aside payments to ordinary creditors that were made within 90 days of the filing of bankruptcy.

- A Trustee may set aside payments made to insiders (relatives, business partners) made within one year prior to the filing of bankruptcy.

- Transfer of money or property to someone outright (not to pay off a debt), whereby the person did not pay fair value, or paid something less than fair value) may be set aside if occurring within two years prior to the bankruptcy. (Note: Bankruptcy Trustees may also use state law, as well, to recover fraudulent conveyances. For example, in Arizona, bankruptcy trustee can set aside any transfer of money or property occurring within four years prior to bankruptcy, because Arizona's law has a longer period of time to look back than the federal Bankruptcy Code. Different states have different fraudulent conveyance statutes permitting additional time to go after people who receive money or property without paying fair value.

- Transfers of property to a self-settled trust within 10 years prior to bankruptcy can be set aside.

It is important to note that certain transfers of property prior to bankruptcy will not be set aside. The following are examples of transfers of money or property prior to bankruptcy, which are not a problem:

- Transfer of an asset to anyone, whereby the person receiving the asset paid fair value. (I.e. debtor sells his boat that is worth $10,000 to his brother for the sum of $10,000. Brother will not lose the boat, as brother paid for it. However, the Trustee may want to see proof of payment and value of the boat. Also, if the sale happened close in time before bankruptcy, the Trustee may ask what happened to the money?)

- Repaying a friend $3,000.00 on a legitimate debt four months before the bankruptcy case was filed. A friend is not a "relative," and the payment was more than 90 days pre-bankruptcy the payment will not be set aside. Payments to "ordinary" creditors may only be set aside if made within 90 days before bankruptcy filing. (However, the Trustee may want proof that a debt was actually owed to the friend.)

- Repaying a relative $10,000.00 thirteen months prior to the bankruptcy filing. Since this is more than one year prior to bankruptcy filing, even though it is a relative, it may not be set aside if it is payment upon a legitimate debt. A Chapter 7 Trustee may try to prove that it really was not repayment of the debt, but rather it was a gift.

- Spending money before filing bankruptcy. While all bankruptcy filings have a "good faith" requirement, spending money before filing your case, or selling an asset and thereafter spending the money, is not a problem. It is your money to spend as you choose. I have had clients who had gambling problems, who admittedly spent lots of money before hitting rock bottom. Although loss of money through gambling is frowned upon, gambling is a legal transaction in certain venues, such that a person is not penalized for bad mistakes. Sometimes these issues will prompt an investigation by the Trustee to assure that the bankruptcy debtor is not being dishonest. He may ask to see hotel receipts to prove that the debtor was really in the casino in Las Vegas on the date of the losses. Additionally, you are required to disclose all such losses as part of the bankruptcy filing.

Bankruptcy affords tremendous relief and a fresh start. The key is to completely disclose ALL required information, and most importantly, do not omit material information. Do not hide assets. Do not lie.

In the Chapter 7 case, the Trustee files a report with the Court informing that the bankruptcy debtor has fully cooperated, made all required financial disclosures, and that a discharge of debts is recommended. The Trustee informs whether or not any assets are being sold to bring money to creditors. (In the great majority of Chapter 7 cases, no assets are sold.) The Bankruptcy Judge thereafter enters a Court Order that all dischargeable debts are eliminated. These debts may not be revived in any way, shape or form in the future. In the event that any nonexempt asset was taken and sold by the Trustee, disbursement checks will go out to creditors. In such cases, creditors will receive an equal percentage of their claims.

It is a violation of the Bankruptcy Court's Order of Discharge for any creditor or debt collector to attempt to collect a debt that has been discharged in bankruptcy. Furthermore, as previously discussed, it is a violation of the Fair Debt Collection Practices Act (FDCPA) for a debt collector or debt buyer to attempt to collect a debt that is been discharged in bankruptcy. Not only can a FDCPA lawsuit be filed for damages, but the Judge of the United States Bankruptcy Court can enter a civil contempt Order for a violation of the Discharge Order. Finally, a creditor who continues to report to credit bureaus that the debt is owed when it has been discharged in bankruptcy violates the Fair Credit Reporting Act (FCRA), which may entitle recovery of damages to the consumer.

A Chapter 7 Bankruptcy case usually takes four to five months to complete, although timetables vary from district to district. The relief and protection of bankruptcy begins the very instant that the case is filed. A Court Order is automatically entered in the case (known as the "automatic stay") which stops any and all collection efforts on the part of any creditor, including lawsuits or legal proceedings. In fact, even if the creditor already obtained a judgment, and wages are being garnished, the moment that the bankruptcy case is filed, no more garnishments or collection efforts may occur. In the event a garnishment happens, the money must be returned to the bankruptcy debtor. Unlike other legal cases, you do not have to wait until the end of the case to get relief. The relief is automatic and immediate as soon as the bankruptcy case filed. Any creditor who neglects to follow these rules can be held in contempt by the Bankruptcy Court. Any effort to try to collect on a debt against a bankruptcy debtor is a willful violation of the automatic stay. Creditors may request to see the judge, by filing a motion that they should be removed from this prohibition, if they have good cause. For example, if the bankruptcy debtor is not making any mortgage payments, or has stopped making car payments, the creditor may ask the Bankruptcy Judge for "relief from the automatic stay," and that the creditor be allowed to recover its collateral through foreclosure or repossession. If a person is behind on mortgage payments or car payments, and wants to keep the property, then a Chapter 13 case should be considered (discussed below).

Once a bankruptcy case is filed, the creditor may not exercise "self-help" remedies, even if the creditor has a Court order out of another court. The Bankruptcy Court's authority supersedes and controls over all other court orders from other courts. (There are a few limited exceptions: Child support and alimony (spousal maintenance) orders remain in effect; Orders from criminal courts are not affected.)

Certain debts will survive a Chapter 7 bankruptcy as a matter of law. Such debts that will not go away include: child support obligations, recent taxes (due within three years before bankruptcy filing), student loans, debts procured through fraud, malicious or willful injury judgments, criminal fines and penalties (restitution orders, traffic tickets, DUI/DWI fines, etc.) If you have issues related to nondischargeable debts, such as taxes and student loans, it is critical that you seek the advice of a competent attorney. Older taxes may be completely eliminated, but only if you meet certain conditions, and only if proper procedures take place in the bankruptcy court. Student loans may be eliminated through special proceedings if the student loans impose an "undue hardship" on the debtor or the debtor's family. Eliminating these additional debts may not be an option if the bankruptcy case is filed without the proper additional documents being filed and necessary proceedings initiated. The rights to eliminate some of these additional debts, such as student loans, can be completely waived if not asserted properly and timely in the bankruptcy case. (For a more detailed comprehensive analysis on reducing or eliminating student loans, read *The Student Loan Debt Relief Playbook*, a Legal Playbooks® publication.

<u>What property is protected?</u>

As previously stated, each state has different rules as to what property is protected in the event of filing bankruptcy. Although the bankruptcy code itself has its own set of "federal exemptions," Congress has allowed the states' legislatures to determine whether or not they chose to allow their citizens to claim these "federal" exemptions. In order to understand what property is protected, you must understand which state's exemptions will apply to the bankruptcy filing.

In 2005, in order to address what Congress perceived to be as ongoing abuses of bankruptcy law, Congress passed significant Bankruptcy Code amendments. One of the perceived abuses was that if a debtor got in trouble with his creditors, the debtor could cash out his assets and run into a state that has great property protections, such as Texas or Florida. These two states have homestead exemptions that are unlimited as to value. There were stories of wealthy debtors melting their gold down into doorknobs, and putting them on the doors in their Florida mansions. Precious gems would be placed into chandeliers and placed in the dining areas of the mansions. The debtor would then have the ability to file bankruptcy, and claim homestead protections as to the components of his home, which include the doors and their doorknobs, the lighting fixtures and chandeliers. Then, after the bankruptcy was over, the gold and precious jewels could be taken out of the home and converted back into cash. In order to deal with this type of abuse, Congress changed the law such that now when a bankruptcy case is filed, a determination is made as to where the Debtor resided two years prior to the bankruptcy case. If the debtor resided in any other state within two years before filing the bankruptcy case, the new bankruptcy law looks to see where that debtor lived the better part of six months before the two year period. Under present law, if a person cashes his assets out in California, and runs over to the

Florida, investing all of his money and assets into a Florida mansion, upon filing bankruptcy, the Court will look to see where the debtor resided two years before the case was filed. In the above example, even though the debtor may file his bankruptcy case in the Florida, the California property protections will apply.

Under the law, a person has the right to migrate to any state within the United States. Furthermore, laws generally permit a person to take their assets with them. However, amendments to the Bankruptcy Code now prevent a person from benefiting in bankruptcy by jumping over to another state.

# Chapter 13 Bankruptcy

Chapter 13 Bankruptcy is available for individuals who are in the upper half of income earners under the “means test.” However, most Chapter 13 cases are filed out of necessity, as Chapter 13 allows a debtor to restructure payments with respect to the debts that are necessary to keep, while at the same time affording the debtor the same discharge of a Chapter 7. In other words, a Chapter 13 bankruptcy eliminates the debts that need to be eliminated, while at the same time presenting a plan to reorganize (restructure) other essential debts. Chapter 13 offers a restructured payment plan on those debts that the debtor needs to keep and pay off (mortgage payments, car payments, tax debts, child support obligations), while at the same time discharging those debts that the debtor cannot afford to pay (credit cards, medical bills, etc.).

When a Chapter 13 bankruptcy is filed, the Chapter 13 case essentially brings all loans into a current status as a matter of law.

If the debtor is behind on his home mortgage or automobile payments, such loans are deemed current at the very moment that the Chapter 13 case is filed. If the car has been repossessed, it must be returned to the debtor. If a foreclosure sale is scheduled, it may not go forward. For this reason, Chapter 13 can be very helpful to stop foreclosures and rehabilitate mortgage problems. Also, Chapter 13 will allow restructuring of automobile payments. In many instances, a vehicle loan may be modified by lowering the contract price down to the value of the vehicle, lowering the interest rate to a reasonable market rate, eliminating missed car payments, and allowing the car to be paid off over a period of up to 60 months. By filing a Chapter 13, unsecured credit card debts may be eliminated, while secured loans may be restructured to make payments more affordable. Also, tax liabilities that cannot be discharged (tax due within three years prior to bankruptcy) can be paid off at zero-interest zero-penalties, affording a tremendous savings to the debtor. Chapter 13 can also allow complete elimination of second mortgages and home equity loans. The rules governing restructuring mortgages and eliminating home-equity lines vary from district to district in the United States. It is necessary that debtors understand the law in the jurisdiction where they reside and will be filing their bankruptcy case, in order to understand the level of relief available. This section provides a brief summary as to the additional things that may be accomplished in a Chapter 13 case that may not be accomplished in through a Chapter 7 filing.

## Mortgages

- Arrears on a mortgage may be paid out over sixty months, and usually at zero interest. (Laws differ from District to District). A case may be filed up until the actual foreclosure sale. If the Chapter 13 case is filed, the foreclosure sale is stopped, and the loan is deemed current under federal law. The Chapter 13 Plan will provide for repayment of the arrears over a term of up to 60 months.

- Second mortgages/home-equity loans may be eliminated in their entirety. This may include home improvement loans, or home-equity lines of credit (HELOCs) (Again, this depends on the law of the District where the bankruptcy case is filed. Also, the value of the home determines whether junior mortgage liens may be "stripped" from the property.)

- Property taxes and Homeowner's Association (HOA) Fees may be cured through the Chapter 13 plan over a period of up to sixty months.

- Judgment liens that impair the homestead property may be removed from the home and discharged as unsecured obligations. (Without bankruptcy, the judgment lien would remain attached to the home). This can also be done in Chapter 7.

## Automobiles

- A Chapter 13 plan may lower the price of the automobile down to its value. In other words, an upside down loan can be reduced down to the value of the collateral. Under present bankruptcy law, this forced "cram down" may only occur if the loan was made more than 2 ½ years prior to the bankruptcy filing.

- If you are behind on car payments, missed car payments are removed. You are not required to catch up. The car will be paid under new terms as set out in your Chapter 13 plan. The new payment will not begin until 30 days after the case is filed.

- Interest rates may be lowered to a market rate. (Market rates at time of this publication are around 7%) Bankruptcy Courts in the United States have different opinions as to what is a "market rate."

- The car can be paid off over a period of up to 60 months.

- If the car was repossessed before bankruptcy, the car must be returned. The debtor does not even have to pay the repo fees.

Lowering the price, lowering the interest rate, and paying off the car over a period of sixty months usually results in a significantly lower monthly payment obligation to pay off the vehicle.

## Taxes

Taxes due within three years prior to the filing of bankruptcy are generally not dischargeable. Older taxes may be completely eliminated, provided that they meet certain requirements. If these requirements are met, taxes due more than three years prior to bankruptcy may be totally eliminated.

Your worst day situation with taxes in Chapter 13 is that they are income taxes of a nature that cannot be eliminated. But there is good news, even in this worst day scenario. To the extent that taxes must be paid, Chapter 13 will allow removal of all penalties in the past, and stop additional penalties in the future. This includes non-filing penalties and all penalties that have been assessed since the time the tax was due. Under Chapter 13, a debtor may then propose to pay the taxes out, along with any interest that accumulated prior to the bankruptcy case, over a period of up to sixty months at zero interest, zero penalty. At the time of this publication, the IRS assesses 22% interest and penalty per year (12% interest, and 10% penalty). The problem for most taxpayers is if they owe a significant amount of taxes, although they may be able to work out a payment plan with the IRS, the ongoing interest and penalty make it next to impossible to ever pay down the tax. Payments that are made are always first applied to outstanding penalties, then to the oldest tax year. Debtors can find themselves in a situation where even if they pay a significant monthly payment for the rest of their life, they are only covering ongoing interest and penalty, with the tax never getting paid. In Chapter 13, the law permits a zero-interest zero-penalty payout, which means that every dollar paid on the IRS claim reduces the tax. There is no additional assessed interest or penalty on any amount due to the tax authority while the tax claim is being paid off over five years.

It is impossible to be completely thorough on the details of dealing with tax claims in this book. There are different types of taxes (i.e. sales taxes, employer 941 taxes, income taxes, etc.). There are different rules for treatment of different types of tax claims. This zero-interest zero-penalty payout is an option available to eliminate income taxes through Chapter 13. Other type of tax claims must be paid with interest, but presently, required interest rates on some other type of tax claims are as low as 4%.

In the event that the tax authority has a recorded tax lien, the tax authority is in a better position with respect to the age of its tax claim. Once a tax lien is filed, the tax debt may not be eliminated in the same manner as if a tax lien had never been filed. If the taxes are "liened," Chapter 13 may permit reduction of the tax lien down to the value of property held by the debtor. If the debtor owns only household goods, and has no equity in the home because of the present market conditions, this means that a tax lien can be reduced down to a very low amount, to be paid inside of the Chapter 13 Plan. This cannot be done outside of a Chapter 13 Bankruptcy case.

Dealing with taxes in bankruptcy is a complex area of the law. I have had a number of clients come to me after they had been represented by another attorney. I found that even many bankruptcy attorneys lack adequate knowledge of dealing with tax claims in bankruptcy. If you have tax claims against you, be sure that you confirm that the attorney you are considering to handle your case has experience an in-depth knowledge with eliminating and/or reducing taxes. I have encountered attorneys who simply have not studied the law to the extent necessary to understand that certain taxes may be completely eliminated, with other taxes substantially reduced and being paid under the most favorable terms (zero interest and penalty). If these concepts seem unfamiliar to an attorney reviewing your case, you should seek out a more experienced attorney.

## Student loans

Prior to 1998, student loans could be fully discharged in bankruptcy, as long as the student loans were more than seven years old. The Clinton Administration received much praise for finding ways to balance the federal budget without raising taxes. This Administration sought out ways to raise revenue by focusing on areas where the federal government was losing money. The end result with respect to student loans was that the law was revised, such that student loans could no longer be discharged in bankruptcy, no matter how old the loans were. This exception to discharge has placed tremendous burden on people who have very old student loans that have doubled, and even tripled, because of ongoing interest charges since the time the debtor received the education. Many of the private schools went out of business and no longer offer job placement services.

At the time of writing of this publication, a Bill is pending in Congress which may cause certain student loans to become dischargeable in bankruptcy. Since the law is not yet passed, I will not detail its provisions here. The expectation is that certain student loans will be fully dischargeable if the loan is more than five years old, if the debtor made reasonable efforts to pay the loan. There is a debate in Congress as to whether or not there should be a different standard for private student loans versus Federal Government student loans. There is certain to be much debate as to the specific areas of this new Bill. The good news is that there is a strong expectation that both Democrats and

Republicans will support some version of the Bill to make it easier to eliminate student loans through Bankruptcy in situations of hardship, and in situations where the loans are very old.

Presently, bankruptcy law only provides one narrow path to eliminate student loans. This is known as the "undue hardship" exception. A debtor in bankruptcy has the right to file an action against the student loan lender to seek to have the Court determine that holding the debtor to the terms of the student loan and not allowing it to be discharged will impose "undue hardship upon the debtor or the debtor's family." The various Circuit Courts in the United States differ in their interpretation of what is required to meet this "undue hardship" exception. In practice, and through interpretation of relevant case law, I have learned that discharging student loans in bankruptcy is a very difficult thing to do.

In most Districts, the "undue hardship" exception to non-dischargeability of student loans requires that essentially three things be shown. First, that based upon current income and expenses, the debtor cannot maintain a minimal standard of living for himself and dependents if forced to repay the student loans; second, such financial situation is likely to continue for a significant part of the repayment period; and third, the debtor has made a "good-faith effort" to repay the student loans. Different Circuit Courts use different tests to determine whether or not student loan should be included in the discharge. Some Courts look at a totality of the circumstances, and focus on whether or not the student is receiving an economic benefit from the education, or will receive economic benefits in the future. Most judicial opinions find that if a person earned a college degree, even if they are not working in the field of their specialty, they have better economic opportunities than if they had not received the degree.

Because there are so many different scenarios that may or may not justify a person receiving an expanded discharge that will eliminate student loans under the "undue hardship" exception, I will not attempt to detail them further here. This is an additional area where you would want to make sure that any attorney who may be retained to handle the bankruptcy case is well familiar with the standard for determining whether or not a student loan may be discharged under the "undue hardship" exception. In the event that the pending bill in Congress is passed, elimination of older student loans shall not require a special litigation and trial against the student loan lender before a bankruptcy judge. Returning to a less oppressive law relating to student loan lenders will provide a path for relief to debtors overwhelmed with student loan debt.

Chapter 13 does permit modification of student loan payments. Some Districts allow the lender to be treated as a special class creditor and to allow the loan to be paid ahead of other debt. Other Districts will not allow the student loan creditor to receive special treatment ahead of other creditors. In any case, the student loans may always be deferred (out of the way) for the entire payment period of the Chapter 13 plan, which means you can focus on getting other essential things paid, without interference from the student loan lender for the entire five year plan.

For a more detailed comprehensive analysis on reducing or eliminating student loans or fighting the student loan creditor, read *The Student Loan Debt Relief Playbook,* a Legal Playbooks® publication.

## Child Support Obligations

Although child support obligations can essentially never be discharged through bankruptcy, Chapter 13 provides a mechanism to allow the child support to be paid over a period of up to sixty months. Most of the time, if a person owes child support arrears, the state court that issued the child support order will fashion a repayment plan which is quite often more than five-year payout. If this is the case, it will usually makes better sense to accept what the State family court has provided, as opposed to paying off the child support obligation inside of a Chapter 13 plan. However, some family courts are less forgiving of parents not paying their child support. I have seen cases where a state family court judge held a parent in contempt for nonpayment of child support, put him in jail, and set a bond amount of the entire child support due. Thereafter, the court would enter an order which allowed the incarcerated parent to leave the jail in the morning to go to work, and come back to the jail after work. In a situation of this kind, where there is a large amount of child support arrearage that is immediately due, and there is some consequence to the debtor if it is not paid immediately, Chapter 13 can help. By filing the Chapter 13 case, the debtor is permitted to pay out the child support obligation over a sixty-month plan. This right is absolute, and cannot be denied by a state family court judge. The child support obligation will get paid ahead of essentially everything else in the payment plan, with limited exceptions.

Most often, a parent owing back child support can get a payment plan from the family law court. Elimination of other debts by filing bankruptcy, combined with a five-year payment plan may assist the child support debtor, where other options have failed.

## Criminal Fines and Penalties

Criminal fines and penalties may be paid out inside of the Chapter 13 plan, again over a period of time of up to sixty months. However, filing a Chapter 13 bankruptcy will not stop any criminal prosecution, where the person has not yet been convicted. Criminal cases shall move forward, but if a criminal fine or penalty is determined, it may be paid through terms established under the Chapter 13 bankruptcy case.

## Credit Card and Other Debts

One of the biggest myths and misguided rumors that I hear from people about Chapter 13, is that they believe that if a Chapter 13 bankruptcy case is filed, they will have to pay off "all of their debts" over five years. This is simply not the case. In fact, in an estimated 90% of cases, a person filing Chapter 13 case can afford to pay no more than the minimum amount necessary to pay off the essentials (mortgage arrears, the car the car at a lower price and lower interest rate, taxes at zero interest zero penalty, etc.) There simply isn't enough income to pay money towards to the unsecured creditors (credit cards, medical bills, etc.) As long as the Chapter 13 Trustee agrees that the debtor cannot afford more than what is necessary to pay off the car, taxes, and any other essential items, the Chapter 13 Plan will be approved with the all unsecured creditors essentially being discharged in full. In fact, in most Chapter 13 cases, the creditors are getting less than they would in Chapter 7. (The IRS's loses its penalties, the car lender loses its excessive interest and underwater portion of the loan, mortgage lenders won't get interest and ongoing late fees on their arrearage claims). The reality is that in most Chapter 13 cases, unsecured creditors are paid little to nothing.

The same Discharge is ordered by the judge in a Chapter 13 case as in a Chapter 7 case. The Discharge eliminates all debts that were not paid by the monthly plan payment. If the debtor is properly represented, the plan payment will not be any higher than what is necessary to pay off essential items, as the income simply is not there to pay more to other creditors. There are special rules that govern Chapter 13. For example, the approved plan payment does depend on the income of the debtor who files a Chapter 13. Furthermore, there are rules that can affect the plan payment, depending on the assets that you own.

## The Chapter 13 Trustee does not seize assets.

Unlike a Chapter 7 Trustee, the Chapter 13 Trustee does not take and sell assets. Chapter 13 allows a debtor to keep all assets, whether they are protected or not. Rather, the Chapter 13 Debtor makes monthly payments to the Chapter 13 Trustee. Although assets cannot be lost, a person who owns nonexempt property that would be lost in a Chapter 7 (i.e. a boat, cash on hand, or other nonexempt property) may be required to pay a higher monthly plan payment, so as to get some money to the unsecured creditors by the end of the payment plan. In such cases, the case may result in discharging 85-90% of the unsecured credit (credit cards medical bills etc.) and paying 10-15% of the debt through the additional amount funded into the sixty-month plan. This is another area that should be discussed with a qualified attorney.

It is very difficult to proceed through a Chapter 13 case without an attorney. However, most attorneys will wait and be paid (at least most of their fees) through the Chapter 13 monthly plan payments. Most attorneys will require some form of up-front payment, with most of the fees to be paid by the court at a future date.

## Filing a Chapter 13 Only Because Over-Mean Income

Some people file under Chapter 13 simply because they make too much money to file a Chapter 7 case. In this situation, the person filing is entitled to receive a discharge to the same extent as they would Chapter 7 case. The difference is that the Chapter 13 Debtor will be required to make some form of the monthly plan payment, but never more than the debtor can afford. Again, monthly income is first dedicated to those assets and debts that must be paid off (mortgage, cars, and taxes). Only to the extent that the Chapter 13 debtor can afford to pay any amount above what is necessary to clear these essential obligations, will the debtor be required to pay towards unsecured debts. The end result is that the Discharge will eliminate a high percentage of the unsecured debts, with a smaller percentage being paid, simply because the income is there to do so.

Chapter 13 puts the debtor in a situation where the debtor, and not the creditor, tells the creditors what they will be paid based upon what the debtor can afford. While creditors can participate and file objections, they generally do not. Creditors understand that the Chapter 13 Trustee will approve a plan payment that is fair, and that they will get whatever they get. It is essential that you have a skilled Chapter 13 attorney handle your case. You will find that many bankruptcy lawyers will tell you that they only handle Chapter 7 cases, and not Chapter 13 cases. Also, you may encounter lawyers who try to have you believe that Chapter 7 is always a better choice. This is not true in most situations. Especially, when you can receive the absolute most relief in a Chapter 13 case by eliminating those debts you need to get rid of, and also adjusting payments on those things that you need to keep and pay off. I find in my practice that even many bankruptcy lawyers do not understand the ability to eliminate second mortgages and home equity lines through Chapter 13. Be sure when you make an appointment with a bankruptcy attorney, you choose on that handles all Chapters of Bankruptcy. This way, you know you are receiving a complete analysis of your debt situation, and that you file the Chapter of Bankruptcy that provides the absolute most relief. You will not be served well if you choose an attorney who only handles Chapter 7 cases (which is the great majority of lawyers who hold themselves out as Bankruptcy attorneys).

# Chapter 11 Bankruptcy

A Chapter 11 Bankruptcy is usually a bankruptcy case that is only filed by a corporation or business entity (such as a limited liability company (LLCs)). Corporations and LLCs are not allowed to file under Chapter 13. Corporations and LLCs may not get a discharge in Chapter 7. Therefore, the only meaningful Chapter to allow a business entity to relieve itself from debt is Chapter 11. Sometimes a Chapter 11 cases will be filed for an individual, in the event that the individual has too much debt to qualify for Chapter 13. To file a Chapter 13 case, a debtor may not have secured loans (mortgages, vehicles loans) that exceed $1,081,400.00, nor may they have unsecured debts (credit cards, medical bills, etc.) exceeding the sum of $360,475.00.

Chapter 11 Bankruptcy, while affording tremendous relief to business entities, is usually not the best choice for an individual. Unlike a Chapter 13 case, creditors have the right to cast a vote as to whether or not they agree to the proposed repayment plan (plan of reorganization). If the required majority does not approve the Plan, the case is dismissed or converted to Chapter 7. (In Chapter 13, one individual (the Trustee) essentially says "yes" or "no" to your proposed payment to creditors, which means that a plan may be approved without the agreement of any creditor.) Getting enough votes from the creditors to accept or reject a plan of reorganization requires much time and effort on the part of the attorney, which translates to significant expense. Most attorneys will require a hefty fee (usually many thousands of dollars) up front to file Chapter 11.

Chapter 11 is usually the last choice for a person whose debts exceed the allowable debt limits of Chapter 13. Chapter 11 will prevent seizure and sale of assets, and where the value of assets justify the considerable expense of the case, it is worthwhile.

If you consult with an attorney regarding the prospective filing of a Chapter 11 Bankruptcy, be prepared to discuss an expensive process. The reason for this is that Chapter 11 requires much more court intervention, filing of motions, and notices to creditors.

Further discussion of Chapter 11 is beyond the scope of this book. In the event my readers need additional information on Chapter 11, I highly recommend a meeting with a Chapter 11 attorney. Most consumer bankruptcy attorneys do not handle Chapter 11 cases. Chapter 11 bankruptcy law is a very specialized area of practice.

## Bankruptcy Planning

So many people follow their knee-jerk reaction and do things that are entirely inappropriate or unnecessary in advance of bankruptcy, out of fear that the creditor will recover their assets. Sadly, most of these reaction-based moves cause more problems. The absolute worst thing that a person can do when their creditors are after them is to transfer money or property to another person. Every state has a fraudulent conveyance statute which provides that in the event that money or property is transferred to another person, without that person paying fair value, that transfer may be set aside. Federal Bankruptcy law also permits bankruptcy trustees to go after the property that was transferred.

There are legitimate transactions in advance of bankruptcy that can prevent loss of assets and income.

## Selling Assets in Advance of Bankruptcy

If a person needs money to survive because they have lost a job or other source of income, and that person needs to sell something, it simply makes sense to sell the asset that would be at risk in a Chapter 7 bankruptcy case. For example, if the debtor owns a boat, or has cash savings, understanding that these items could potentially be lost in a Chapter 7 Bankruptcy (depending on the applicable state or federal exemption statutes), it simply makes sense to sell these items first. Be prepared to disclose these sales and transfers at a later time. There is no penalty to the debtor for selling property that the debtor owns. It is his to sell. In fact, even if the debtor sells the asset for less than fair value, it does not present a problem to the debtor, only to the person purchasing the property. Innocent purchasers are protected. Of course, any sales or transfers in advance of bankruptcy must be properly disclosed at the time the bankruptcy case is filed. Simply put, you are not in trouble for selling your own property before bankruptcy.

Wait, and do not cash out or transfer assets that are protected. Sadly, I have seen people come into my law firm for bankruptcy advice who were so fearful of their creditors, that they transferred their home into an irrevocable trust or to another person. The home was protected under the homestead statute, but the protection was lost with the property transferred away. Transferring property that is protected under law results in losing the protection, as you cannot claim the protection on property you no longer own. Likewise, it is a mistake to cash out a retirement plan that is protected while in the plan, but which is not protected after withdrawal.

Be sure and gain a proper understanding of property protections (exemptions) before transferring assets or converting protected property to non-protected property.

## Transferring Sentimental or Important Assets to Family Members Before Bankruptcy

Again, as long as the person receiving the property pays fair value, transfers to relatives or any person for that matter is fine, and will not be set aside. The Bankruptcy Trustee will request proof of a valid sale (usually a copy of the check used to purchase the item, and proof that the check was actually deposited in the debtor's account – funds transferred). Likewise, it is fine to repurchase the asset from the family member after the bankruptcy is over. As long as each transaction was a legitimate sale, for fair value, and as long as it was properly disclosed, there is no loss of the asset or problem with the bankruptcy trustee.

<u>Example:</u> Before filing bankruptcy, father sells boat worth $5,000.00 to son for $5,000.00 and has evidence that son paid for the boat. Father spends $5,000.00 down on living expenses within two months prior to bankruptcy. Father files bankruptcy, and makes full disclosure of the transaction. Since this was a bona fide sale for value, son keeps the boat. Father later buys back the boat from son. This is perfectly fine.

## Paying off a Friendly Creditor in Advance of Bankruptcy

The debtor filing bankruptcy is not in trouble for paying off a debt in advance of bankruptcy. The only issue is whether or not the payment may be set aside. As long as 90 days pass from the time of payment before bankruptcy, the ordinary creditor (non-relative) will get to keep the payment. As long as one year passes from the date of payment to the relative or insider, the relative or insider will get to keep the payment. The issue that may be reviewed is whether or not the payment was really for a legitimate debt. The debtor may have to establish through some documentation that he really owed the debt to the family member. Otherwise, the Trustee will urge the Court to consider the payment to be a gift, and try to get the money back. In establishing whether or not the payment was really for a legitimate debt, the trustee may ask for proof that money was actually advanced by the relative at the time that the loan was purported to have been made.

# Bankruptcy for Non-U.S. Citizens

A non-citizen may file a Bankruptcy case in the United States. Generally, all that is required is that the non-citizen has "an asset" located within the United States. This can be a bank account with a small balance. A great number of nations of the world have entered into treaties with the United States, which require respect and enforcement of Judgments rendered in the United States. Interestingly, foreign countries, whose laws do not permit bankruptcy relief or whose laws are much more oppressive towards debtors, have agreed by treaty to respect and enforce

United States Court Orders, which include Bankruptcy Discharge Orders. Recently, I heard a bankruptcy practitioner at a legal seminar comment that "Bankruptcy has become one of the United States' biggest exports!" Many overseas corporations have sought protection from their creditors by filing their bankruptcy cases in the United States. As to consumers, it is generally required that the debtor establish identity, through a government issued photo ID, which can be a TIN number or other acceptable identifying document. In the context of consumer case, the debtor or the debtor's spouse need not be a citizen of the United States to receive a bankruptcy discharge.

## A Fresh Start

Bankruptcy is the one sure way to guarantee relief from your creditors. However, the bankruptcy case must be planned and handled effectively. An improperly managed bankruptcy case can result in loss of assets (Chapter 7) or a higher than necessary monthly plan payment (Chapter 13). By understanding the rules of law that govern creditors' rights, and by fully understanding the powers of the bankruptcy trustees, a debtor can emerge from the bankruptcy process without losing any income or property. A properly handled bankruptcy case will assure that the debtor receives a fresh start, defeating creditors' efforts to seize assets and disable the family.

# Chapter 11

# Credit Counseling and Debt Settlement

I wish I could say that services offering Credit Counseling and/or Debt Settlement would provide solutions that would help people solve their debt problems. However, in my twenty-one years of practice, I have seen only disappointment with respect to people who engaged in such programs. While I encourage my readers to explore all options, which may include debt counseling or true debt settlement efforts, I want you to be aware of things that agencies who operate these businesses will not tell you. First of all, when they claim they are "nonprofit" entities, this simply means that their shareholders are not receiving dividends. Nonprofit corporations can pay their employees (which include their officers and directors) any salary they choose. They simply do not disburse dividends to the shareholder owners. Nonprofit status can be misleading, as it suggests that the agency is government owned, or otherwise managed by a charity. Trust me, they are not.

## Debt Settlement Companies

So-called "Debt Settlement Companies" are a complete waste of time and money. These companies create false hope in the mind of the consumer that they can settle your debt for pennies on the dollar. They cannot do anything that you cannot do yourself! There are no laws available that enable these so-called "negotiators" to do a better job than you can. If a debt is in default, and the debt is aging due to a long period of time passing, you can accomplish the same thing that these companies would offer for you, by making proposals to the creditor to settle the debt for a lower amount. If you do not have cash reserve, you are wasting time. Creditors do not tend offer lower payments or better payment terms. Debt settlement is effective only if you have some money to work with. Obviously, you do not want to tell the creditor that you have money. If you are attempting to settle your debts, you can let them know that you have someone who is willing to help you on a one-time basis, and that you will only settle the debt for a one-time cash settlement (I have almost always been successful in settling debt for an amount between 40 to 50% of the debt or lower, as long as money was available to make a one-time cash payment. I am the first one to tell my clients that debt settlement companies are not worth the money they charge. If you want a true "debt settlement" helper, work with the bankruptcy attorney who will try to settle the debt to avoid filing bankruptcy. The fees you pay will not be substantial, and will be money well spent. Creditors are much more apt to take you seriously, when they understand you have already employed a bankruptcy lawyer. Also, many bankruptcy attorneys will give you credit for money you paid in the attempt to settle the debt towards a bankruptcy case, if debt settlement is not successful, and you must file a bankruptcy case.

# Credit Counseling Services

The problem with employing credit counseling agencies arises from what they do not disclose to you. These agencies will lead the consumer to believe that they are only charging a nominal fee (often $25-$35 per month) for their services. However, they are not telling you what the creditors are paying for their services. When a credit counseling program is set up, the credit counseling service contacts the creditor and informs, "We have been contacted by a debtor who holds your account. We're going to help collect this debt for you. Our fee is 50% of all money that comes through our program... and by the way, we get 100% of the first 6 payments." While I do not have a problem with the fact that a percentage-of-the-debt fee is charged, I do have a problem with the fact that this fee arrangement is not disclosed to the consumer who has entered the credit counseling program. Credit counseling services cannot do anything to improve credit standing, or even to cause positive information to be reflected on credit reports. In fact, paying through a credit counseling program means that the debt will get many more months in default, and will remain in default while the creditor is receiving only a small percentage of the debt that it would be receiving if the payments were coming through as required under the contract. Accordingly, credit scores are dramatically affected downwardly while participating in these programs. More importantly, the credit counselor cannot prevent you from being sued on the debt. At least every other month I have a person come to my office, who gives me the following story: "I don't understand. We have been paying our monthly payment through our credit counseling service for ten months now. We just got served with a lawsuit. How can this happen?" Credit counselors can do nothing to prevent lawsuits from being filed, other than to try to encourage the creditor not to sue. The problem is that when the credit counseling service is trying to manage 20 debts, maybe 16 out of the 20 creditors will inform that "Yes, we understand and we will accept lower payments. And, we agree to pay your 50% fee, as we understand that if we were sending the case out to collection we would have to pay that anyway." The problem is that two or three of the 20 creditors will either not agree to the terms of the credit counseling service, or otherwise, they won't respond to the phone calls of the credit counselor. So... the lawsuit gets filed anyway. And it only takes one lawsuit, followed by a judgment, followed by one wage garnishment, to force the consumer into bankruptcy.

I have had a number of people in my office who stated that they did find a credit counseling service that was able to hold off creditors for a period of time. Their view was that they did not care if the credit counseling service was receiving a large percentage of the debt, as the service did manage to effectively hold the creditors off under a reasonable payment plan with a reduced rate of interest. Because I have had certain people inform me that they had positive results with certain credit counseling services, I want to be careful and not suggest that all credit counseling services are ineffective. My best advice in determining whether or not a credit counseling service is worth considering, is that you must ask yourself "Is my problem solved if I can manage this debt over a six-year payout, as opposed to a nine year payout?" Reducing interest rates and payments only allows you to continue to defer the problem to another day. The reality is that a significant portion of income, which is needed for necessary living expenses, will be diverted into these programs, and keep the consumer from maintaining an adequate level of support while struggling to meet payments under these plans. I usually recommend that if you are going to enter into a credit counseling service plan, that you also take the opportunity to attend a free consultation with a competent bankruptcy attorney. Advice is free. Get the information. That way, you can make wise decisions.

# Chapter 12

## Hope for a New Day

After twenty-one years of practicing law as a consumer advocate and debt relief attorney, I have learned to pay attention to common trends. Although times change, there seems to have always been a common component with respect to credit card issuers and collectors in how they operate. Literally thousands of times, I have had a desperate consumer in my office going to painstaking lengths to explain how he or she got into trouble with debt. The great majority of people whom I have had the pleasure to meet want to do anything possible to pay off their debts. They recognize and appreciate that the debt they incurred is a legal obligation. I hear more often than one might believe, "I want to pay these debts. I signed for them. I owe them. I want to pay them." The problem is that circumstances of life do not entirely rest within our control. In modern times, most people do not retain their jobs through retirement, as their parents and grandparents may have done. I would say that it is next to impossible for any person to make it through thirty years of mortgage payments, without having some event occur in their life that financially disrupts their ability to meet obligations.

The problem is that creditors and banks, by definition, have a brain but no heart. Bankers get fired if they put money in vaults, and do not earn the highest rate of interest attainable in the marketplace. Any time a bank or lending institution is faced with a decision, the only concern is "What is in the best interest of the

Bank?" The decision makers within the boardrooms of the banks and credit card lenders absolutely refuse, as a matter of policy, to let emotion or regard for their fellow man enter into the discussion. Those at the top level of these companies will tell you that it is "sound business practice," and that the bank's only reason for existence is to "make money." To make matters worse, in recent time, banks and lenders began to engage in business that went way beyond lending their depositors' money to other customers of the bank. Lenders began selling shares of stock, bundled mortgages and debt packages, in the stock market. Now they are dealing with more than decisions that involve the so-called "best interest of the Bank." In taking money from investors, and lending it out, these financial institutions reap their profits based on utilization of other people's money. By lending other people's money, these institutions have justified their way of thinking, and that they have some fiduciary responsibility to make the most money possible to please the shareholders. So after twenty-one years of being asked by the consumer who so desperately wants to pay off her debts, "Why won't they work with me?," I regrettably understand.

Not long ago, I was at a legal education seminar and had the opportunity to meet an attorney employed by the United States Federal Trade Commission. I asked him the same question. "Why doesn't the credit card industry work with more of these debtors, as opposed to seeking judgments and wage garnishments?" It seemed to me that the creditors would lose more money by a debtor filing bankruptcy and wiping the debt away. At least if they worked with the debtor, lowering minimum payments or lowering the interest rate, they would recover much more money than if they push the consumer over the edge into bankruptcy. The answer that this knowledgeable FTC attorney told me may shock you. He explained to me the following: Credit card companies do not pay attention to any one customer. They are only concerned about the profit that they receive from lending money. They understand that they can choose to put money out through different types of lending, and through different types of loans. If they lend the money to the Federal Government (government bonds), they will make between .5% to 2%, with little to no risk. If they elect to loan money to a person who wishes to purchase a home, they will make a return of somewhere between 3.5 to 4.5%, with very little risk of loss of any default. If they choose to lend money out to people who wish to purchase vehicles, they might receive a higher interest rate between 6 to 9%, with a slightly higher risk. State legislatures now permit credit card companies to make unsecured loans to consumers which can range 29.9% and higher. When credit card companies loan money, they give different people different rates. Some people pay 29%. Some people pay a promotional rate of 7 to 9%. Some get 0%. Some get cash back! The bottom line is that if you look at all of the billions of dollars that the credit card issuer sent out to consumer in 2019, the average return on all of the billions of dollars lent through credit cards was 21.25%. The credit card lenders already know that 1.79% of all money loaned out to consumers through credit cards will never come back. This is the result of people who just can't pay, and because of bankruptcy filings. The credit card industry accepts this level of loss, for the reason that they are only focusing on the net numbers. If the average interest earnings on upon all of the billions of dollars is 21.25%, and the default rate is 1.79%, this means that credit card issuers/banks made an average **19.46% profit** on the billions of dollars of business done that year. The credit card industry has been approached by lawmakers who have suggested that laws could be strengthened for purposes of reducing the 1.79% loss rate to a lower number, provided that the credit card issuers would agree to charge lower interest rates to everyone. How do you think the credit card companies responded to this proposal? Of course, they don't want anything changed. Credit card companies fully accept the fact that they may not collect debts because of people who can't pay or because of people who file bankruptcy. It is for this reason that you almost never see a credit card company show up to a meeting in a bankruptcy case. Their general reaction is to close their file once they receive notice of a bankruptcy filing. In certain types of bankruptcy cases, they might file a Proof of Claim informing the Bankruptcy Court of the amount of debt that is owed, in the event that money is recovered.

There have been proposals made at board meetings of the credit card issuers in banks to create loss prevention programs. Responsible employees of credit card companies have proposed, "Why don't we invest a few million dollars in a credit counseling division, and have trained counselors talk to consumers in trouble, in order to reduce the losses?" Quite simply, the credit card companies have had no interest in undertaking any real effort to reduce their losses, because again, there are no overall losses to the bank when it is earning a higher rate of interest than it can in any other investment area available. No other investment available, with an acceptable risk, will produce a certainty of almost 20% annual earnings. The problem for the credit card issuer is that as time moves on, and the credit card companies continue to be unwavering to help people who are in trouble because of the loss of jobs and income, that loss percentage will begin to increase. In fact, it already has climbed significantly since my conversation with the FTC attorney.

I hear story after story of how consumers in trouble spend literally hours on the phone trying to work out payment agreements with their creditors. I consistently hear that they feel like the person on the other end of the phone has no authority to do anything. Much the time, it seems that the credit card company's employee is simply reading from a prepared script, and typing notes into the computer system, reminding the consumer that the call is being recorded. Perhaps if the credit card companies continue to sustain increased levels of losses, they will be forced to react. When their profits go down, they only have two choices: raise interest rates, or to work out plans with debtors who are in trouble. Hopefully, we can begin to elect public officials who will acknowledge the problem, and place some of the responsibility on the credit card companies to counsel with their customers, to work out acceptable options. Losses can be significantly reduced, if creditors would undertake to invest in employees whose job functions are to work towards an agreeable resolution with the debtor. The problem is, the last time I checked, many politicians were attending big parties sponsored by the banks and credit card companies.

Personally, I have always felt that a thirty-year mortgage should include one to two additional years, which can be broken up into months as "payment holidays." If a person has a traumatic event that occurs in his or her life, such as the loss of a job or a medical problem, that person should be able to use one or more months of a "payment holiday." My son, who is in fifth grade, reported to me that his teacher hands out "homework passes," which can be used to skip a homework assignment when necessary. He usually saves them for when he is home sick from school. Of course, the fifth graders homework passes have to be earned through completing extra credit assignments. It would seem that mortgage lenders would include this type of relief within their mortgages. In the present day, mortgage lenders are now writing forty-year mortgages! How can they possibly believe that forty years can pass in the person's life without some significant financial event occurring? Right now, the only guaranteed way to rehabilitate a mortgage default is through a Chapter 13 Bankruptcy case. The fifth grade teacher's idea is a good proposal.

There are many ideas and proposals they could prevent permanent loss and damage to the family because of an unexpected event that produces financial distress. Unfortunately, creditors have not stepped up to the plate to voluntarily create programs to assist people in trouble. Quite frankly, to work out a proposal between debtor and creditor would always result in a win-win situation. To refuse to work with debtors to recover losses to the bank, reminds me of a wealthy person who engages in wasteful spending and squandering, simply because money continues to roll in. If lenders won't act, our lawmakers should. If they won't, vote them out!

Wouldn't it be great if banks and creditors would have a heart? I believe it is an impossible dream, even if lawmakers were to force creditors to consider the consumer circumstances. Look at the failure of the home mortgage work out programs that were designed to help people restructure their mortgages.

I doubt that in my lifetime, we will see banks began to have heart. However, I do believe in the power of the American people to serve as watchdogs over their legislators, urging them to advance consumer protection before the American Dream becomes only a topic of historical discussion of America and its past.

Hopefully, this book has served to inspire those of you who struggle each day for your family's welfare to stand up to creditors and collectors who have no regard for the survival and well-being of you and your family. I urge you to employ those tools under federal and state law to counter their illicit efforts. Also, I hope you will seek out and find an attorney who holds these principles dear, and has dedicated his or her life to taking a stand for justice, and defending the American dream. Although hard to find, when you find this attorney, you will take comfort in the fact that you have a lasting relationship with someone who cares and who will stand by you in difficult times to see justice prevail.

When it comes down to it, the only one person you can completely trust is yourself. You must equip yourself with knowledge of the law in order to prevent becoming a victim, when there is a clear path to victory. The good news is that the law is now at your fingertips. No longer must you go to a lawyer to understand your basic legal rights. With powerful resources, such as the internet and informative publications, you have the tools to battle and defeat the unwary creditor.

"We shall defend our island, whatever the cost may be, we shall fight on the beaches, we shall fight on the landing grounds, we shall fight in the fields and in the streets, we shall fight in the hills; we shall never surrender." *Winston Churchill*

"Better to fight for something than live for nothing." *George S. Patton*

"It's not the size of the dog in the fight, it's the size of the fight in the dog." *Mark Twain.*

"Fight, Fight, FIGHT! And when they come at you again, finish the fight!" *Mark Wesbrooks*

# The War Chest

# Appendix

The attached letters and court documents are samples, and nothing more. Forms and sample documents can never replace the skill training and sound judgment of a qualified attorney. By furnishing these sample documents, it is not intended to provide any legal advice, or to otherwise suggest any matter stated within the samples may apply to the reader's actual legal issue. The sample forms are designed to assist in a basic understanding of framing issues, notifying the adversary creditor, and to provide a sample form of drafting with respect to court pleadings.

## 50 STATES PHONE RECORDING RULES

**One party to the conversation must be aware of the recording in the following States (if so, the call may be recorded) <u>This means you can record as you are the "one party" aware of the recording.</u>:**

Alabama
Alaska
Arizona
Arkansas
Colorado
District Of Columbia
Georgia
Hawaii
Idaho
Illinois
Indiana
Iowa
Kansas
Kentucky
Louisiana
Maine
Minnesota
Mississippi
Missouri
Nebraska
New Jersey
New Mexico
New York
North Carolina
North Dakota
Oklahoma
Oregon
Ohio
Rhode Island
South Carolina
South Dakota
Tennessee

Texas
Utah
Vermont
Virginia
West Virginia
Wisconsin
Wyoming

**States Requiring that Each Party be Aware that the Call is being Recorded (must inform each party that conversation is being recorded):**

California
Connecticut
Delaware
Florida
Massachusetts
Maryland
Michigan
Montana
Nevada
New Hampshire
Pennsylvania
Washington

Remember that laws change, and specific requirements vary. For example, some states prohibit recording of certain types of caller or by certain callers. Most states prohibit attorneys recording calls for purpose of securing evidence for an anticipated legal proceeding. These rules extend to persons acting on behalf of an attorney or person anticipating litigation. The bottom line: Be sure you understand your State's rules on recording calls. Some states have stiff penalties for violating these laws. For example: Recording a phone call without consent is a felony in Nevada, punishable by up to four years in prison and/or $2,000 in fines.

## THE FAIR DEBT COLLECTION PRACTICES ACT

**As amended by Public Law 104-208, 110 Stat. 3009 (Sept. 30, 1996)**

To amend the Consumer Credit Protection Act to prohibit abusive practices by debt collectors.

Be it enacted by the Senate and House of Representatives of the United States of America in Congress assembled, That the Consumer Credit Protection Act (15 U.S.C. 1601 et seq.) is amended by adding at the end thereof the following new title:

### § 801. Short Title [15 USC 1601 note]

This title may be cited as the "Fair Debt Collection Practices Act."

### § 802. Congressional findings and declarations of purpose [15 USC 1692]

(a) There is abundant evidence of the use of abusive, deceptive, and unfair debt collection practices by many debt collectors. Abusive debt collection practices contribute to the number of personal bankruptcies, to marital instability, to the loss of jobs, and to invasions of individual privacy.

(b) Existing laws and procedures for redressing these injuries are inadequate to protect consumers.

(c) Means other than misrepresentation or other abusive debt collection practices are available for the effective collection of debts.

(d) Abusive debt collection practices are carried on to a substantial extent in interstate commerce and through means and instrumentalities of such commerce. Even where abusive debt collection practices are purely intrastate in character, they nevertheless directly affect interstate commerce.

(e) It is the purpose of this title to eliminate abusive debt collection practices by debt collectors, to insure that those debt collectors who refrain from using abusive debt collection practices are not competitively disadvantaged, and to promote consistent State action to protect consumers against debt collection abuses.

**§ 803. Definitions [15 USC 1692a]**

As used in this title --

(1) The term "Commission" means the Federal Trade Commission.

(2) The term "communication" means the conveying of information regarding a debt directly or indirectly to any person through any medium.

(3) The term "consumer" means any natural person obligated or allegedly obligated to pay any debt.

(4) The term "creditor" means any person who offers or extends credit creating a debt or to whom a debt is owed, but such term does not include any person to the extent that he receives an assignment or transfer of a debt in default solely for the purpose of facilitating collection of such debt for another.

(5) The term "debt" means any obligation or alleged obligation of a consumer to pay money arising out of a transaction in which the money, property, insurance or services which are the subject of the transaction are primarily for personal, family, or household purposes, whether or not such obligation has been reduced to judgment.

(6) The term "debt collector" means any person who uses any instrumentality of interstate commerce or the mails in any business the principal purpose of which is the collection of any debts, or who regularly collects or attempts to collect, directly or indirectly, debts owed or due or asserted to be owed or due another. Notwithstanding the exclusion provided by clause (F) of the last sentence of this paragraph, the term includes any creditor who, in the process of collecting his own debts, uses any name other than his own which would indicate that a third person is collecting or attempting to collect such debts. For the purpose of section 808(6), such term also includes any person who uses any instrumentality of interstate commerce or the mails in any business the principal purpose of which is the enforcement of security interests. The term does not include --

(A) any officer or employee of a creditor while, in the name of the creditor, collecting debts for such creditor;

(B) any person while acting as a debt collector for another person, both of whom are related by common ownership or affiliated by corporate control, if the person acting as a debt collector does so only for persons to whom it is so related or affiliated and if the principal business of such person is not the collection of debts;

(C) any officer or employee of the United States or any State to the extent that collecting or attempting to collect any debt is in the performance of his official duties;

(D) any person while serving or attempting to serve legal process on any other person in connection with the judicial enforcement of any debt;

(E) any nonprofit organization which, at the request of consumers, performs bona fide consumer credit counseling and assists consumers in the liquidation of their debts by receiving payments from such consumers and distributing such amounts to creditors; and

(F) any person collecting or attempting to collect any debt owed or due or asserted to be owed or due another to the extent such activity (i) is incidental to a bona fide fiduciary obligation or a bona fide escrow arrangement; (ii) concerns a debt which was originated by such person; (iii) concerns a debt which was not in default at the time it was obtained by such person; or (iv) concerns a debt obtained by such person as a secured party in a commercial credit transaction involving the creditor.

(7) The term "location information" means a consumer's place of abode and his telephone number at such place, or his place of employment.

(8) The term "State" means any State, territory, or possession of the United States, the District of Columbia, the Commonwealth of Puerto Rico, or any political subdivision of any of the foregoing.

**§ 804. Acquisition of location information [15 USC 1692b]**

Any debt collector communicating with any person other than the consumer for the purpose of acquiring location information about the consumer shall --

(1) identify himself, state that he is confirming or correcting location information concerning the consumer, and, only if expressly requested, identify his employer;

(2) not state that such consumer owes any debt;

(3) not communicate with any such person more than once unless requested to do so by such person or unless the debt collector reasonably believes that the earlier response of such person is erroneous or incomplete and that such person now has correct or complete location information;

(4) not communicate by post card;

(5) not use any language or symbol on any envelope or in the contents of any communication effected by the mails or telegram that indicates that the debt collector is in the debt collection business or that the communication relates to the collection of a debt; and

(6) after the debt collector knows the consumer is represented by an attorney with regard to the subject debt and has knowledge of, or can readily ascertain, such attorney's name and address, not communicate with any person other than that attorney, unless the attorney fails to respond within a reasonable period of time to the communication from the debt collector.

**]§ 805. Communication in connection with debt collection [15 USC 1692c]**

(a) COMMUNICATION WITH THE CONSUMER GENERALLY. Without the prior consent of the consumer given directly to the debt collector or the express permission of a court of competent jurisdiction, a debt collector may not communicate with a consumer in connection with the collection of any debt --

(1) at any unusual time or place or a time or place known or which should be known to be inconvenient to the consumer. In the absence of knowledge of circumstances to the contrary, a debt collector shall assume that the convenient time for communicating with a consumer is after 8 o'clock antemeridian and before 9 o'clock postmeridian, local time at the consumer's location;

(2) if the debt collector knows the consumer is represented by an attorney with respect to such debt and has knowledge of, or can readily ascertain, such attorney's name and address, unless the attorney fails to respond within a reasonable period of time to a communication from the debt collector or unless the attorney consents to direct communication with the consumer; or

(3) at the consumer's place of employment if the debt collector knows or has reason to know that the consumer's employer prohibits the consumer from receiving such communication.

(b) COMMUNICATION WITH THIRD PARTIES. Except as provided in section 804, without the prior consent of the consumer given directly to the debt collector, or the express permission of a court of competent jurisdiction, or as reasonably necessary to effectuate a postjudgment judicial remedy, a debt collector may not communicate, in connection with the collection of any debt, with any person other than a consumer, his attorney, a consumer reporting agency if otherwise permitted by law, the creditor, the attorney of the creditor, or the attorney of the debt collector.

(c) CEASING COMMUNICATION. If a consumer notifies a debt collector in writing that the consumer refuses to pay a debt or that the consumer wishes the debt collector to cease further communication with the consumer, the debt collector shall not communicate further with the consumer with respect to such debt, except --

(1) to advise the consumer that the debt collector's further efforts are being terminated;

(2) to notify the consumer that the debt collector or creditor may invoke specified remedies which are ordinarily invoked by such debt collector or creditor; or

(3) where applicable, to notify the consumer that the debt collector or creditor intends to invoke a specified remedy.

If such notice from the consumer is made by mail, notification shall be complete upon receipt.

(d) For the purpose of this section, the term "consumer" includes the consumer's spouse, parent (if the consumer is a minor), guardian, executor, or administrator.

**§ 806. Harassment or abuse [15 USC 1692d]**

A debt collector may not engage in any conduct the natural consequence of which is to harass, oppress, or abuse any person in connection with the collection of a debt. Without limiting the general application of the foregoing, the following conduct is a violation of this section:

(1) The use or threat of use of violence or other criminal means to harm the physical person, reputation, or property of any person.

(2) The use of obscene or profane language or language the natural consequence of which is to abuse the hearer or reader.

(3) The publication of a list of consumers who allegedly refuse to pay debts, except to a consumer reporting agency or to persons meeting the requirements of section 603(f) or 604(3)1 of this Act.

(4) The advertisement for sale of any debt to coerce payment of the debt.

(5) Causing a telephone to ring or engaging any person in telephone conversation repeatedly or continuously with intent to annoy, abuse, or harass any person at the called number.

(6) Except as provided in section 804, the placement of telephone calls without meaningful disclosure of the caller's identity.

**§ 807. False or misleading representations [15 USC 1692e]**

A debt collector may not use any false, deceptive, or misleading representation or means in connection with the collection of any debt. Without limiting the general application of the foregoing, the following conduct is a violation of this section:

(1) The false representation or implication that the debt collector is vouched for, bonded by, or affiliated with the United States or any State, including the use of any badge, uniform, or facsimile thereof.

(2) The false representation of --

(A) the character, amount, or legal status of any debt; or

(B) any services rendered or compensation which may be lawfully received by any debt collector for the collection of a debt.

(3) The false representation or implication that any individual is an attorney or that any communication is from an attorney.

(4) The representation or implication that nonpayment of any debt will result in the arrest or imprisonment of any person or the seizure, garnishment, attachment, or sale of any property or wages of any person unless such action is lawful and the debt collector or creditor intends to take such action.

(5) The threat to take any action that cannot legally be taken or that is not intended to be taken.

(6) The false representation or implication that a sale, referral, or other transfer of any interest in a debt shall cause the consumer to --

(A) lose any claim or defense to payment of the debt; or

(B) become subject to any practice prohibited by this title.

(7) The false representation or implication that the consumer committed any crime or other conduct in order to disgrace the consumer.

(8) Communicating or threatening to communicate to any person credit information which is known or which should be known to be false, including the failure to communicate that a disputed debt is disputed.

(9) The use or distribution of any written communication which simulates or is falsely represented to be a document authorized, issued, or approved by any court, official, or agency of the United States or any State, or which creates a false impression as to its source, authorization, or approval.

(10) The use of any false representation or deceptive means to collect or attempt to collect any debt or to obtain information concerning a consumer.

(11) The failure to disclose in the initial written communication with the consumer and, in addition, if the initial communication with the consumer is oral, in that initial oral communication, that the debt collector is attempting to collect a debt and that any information obtained will be used for that purpose, and the failure to disclose in subsequent communications that the communication is from a debt collector, except that this paragraph shall not apply to a formal pleading made in connection with a legal action.

(12) The false representation or implication that accounts have been turned over to innocent purchasers for value.

(13) The false representation or implication that documents are legal process.

(14) The use of any business, company, or organization name other than the true name of the debt collector's business, company, or organization.

(15) The false representation or implication that documents are not legal process forms or do not require action by the consumer.

(16) The false representation or implication that a debt collector operates or is employed by a consumer reporting agency as defined by section 603(f) of this Act.

**§ 808. Unfair practices [15 USC 1692f]**

A debt collector may not use unfair or unconscionable means to collect or attempt to collect any debt. Without limiting the general application of the foregoing, the following conduct is a violation of this section:

(1) The collection of any amount (including any interest, fee, charge, or expense incidental to the principal obligation) unless such amount is expressly authorized by the agreement creating the debt or permitted by law.

(2) The acceptance by a debt collector from any person of a check or other payment instrument postdated by more than five days unless such person is notified in writing of the debt collector's intent to deposit such check or instrument not more than ten nor less than three business days prior to such deposit.

(3) The solicitation by a debt collector of any postdated check or other postdated payment instrument for the purpose of threatening or instituting criminal prosecution.

(4) Depositing or threatening to deposit any postdated check or other postdated payment instrument prior to the date on such check or instrument.

(5) Causing charges to be made to any person for communications by concealment of the true purpose of the communication. Such charges include, but are not limited to, collect telephone calls and telegram fees.

(6) Taking or threatening to take any nonjudicial action to effect dispossession or disablement of property if --

(A) there is no present right to possession of the property claimed as collateral through an enforceable security interest;

(B) there is no present intention to take possession of the property; or

(C) the property is exempt by law from such dispossession or disablement.

(7) Communicating with a consumer regarding a debt by post card.

(8) Using any language or symbol, other than the debt collector's address, on any envelope when communicating with a consumer by use of the mails or by telegram, except that a debt collector may use his business name if such name does not indicate that he is in the debt collection business.

**§ 809. Validation of debts [15 USC 1692g]**

(a) Within five days after the initial communication with a consumer in connection with the collection of any debt, a debt collector shall, unless the following information is contained in the initial communication or the consumer has paid the debt, send the consumer a written notice containing --

(1) the amount of the debt;

(2) the name of the creditor to whom the debt is owed;

(3) a statement that unless the consumer, within thirty days after receipt of the notice, disputes the validity of the debt, or any portion thereof, the debt will be assumed to be valid by the debt collector;

(4) a statement that if the consumer notifies the debt collector in writing within the thirty-day period that the debt, or any portion thereof, is disputed, the debt collector will obtain verification of the debt or a copy of a judgment against the consumer and a copy of such verification or judgment will be mailed to the consumer by the debt collector; and

(5) a statement that, upon the consumer's written request within the thirty-day period, the debt collector will provide the consumer with the name and address of the original creditor, if different from the current creditor.

(b) If the consumer notifies the debt collector in writing within the thirty-day period described in subsection (a) that the debt, or any portion thereof, is disputed, or that the consumer requests the name and address of the original creditor, the debt collector shall cease collection of the debt, or any disputed portion thereof, until the debt collector obtains verification of the debt or any copy of a judgment, or the name and address of the original creditor, and a copy of such verification or judgment, or name and address of the original creditor, is mailed to the consumer by the debt collector.

(c) The failure of a consumer to dispute the validity of a debt under this section may not be construed by any court as an admission of liability by the consumer.

**§ 810. Multiple debts [15 USC 1692h]**

If any consumer owes multiple debts and makes any single payment to any debt collector with respect to such debts, such debt collector may not apply such payment to any debt which is disputed by the consumer and, where applicable, shall apply such payment in accordance with the consumer's directions.

**§ 811. Legal actions by debt collectors [15 USC 1692i]**

(a) Any debt collector who brings any legal action on a debt against any consumer shall --

(1) in the case of an action to enforce an interest in real property securing the consumer's obligation, bring such action only in a judicial district or similar legal entity in which such real property is located; or

(2) in the case of an action not described in paragraph (1), bring such action only in the judicial district or similar legal entity --

(A) in which such consumer signed the contract sued upon; or

(B) in which such consumer resides at the commencement of the action.

(b) Nothing in this title shall be construed to authorize the bringing of legal actions by debt collectors.

**§ 812. Furnishing certain deceptive forms [15 USC 1692j]**

(a) It is unlawful to design, compile, and furnish any form knowing that such form would be used to create the false belief in a consumer that a person other than the creditor of such consumer is participating in the collection of or in an attempt to collect a debt such consumer allegedly owes such creditor, when in fact such person is not so participating.

(b) Any person who violates this section shall be liable to the same extent and in the same manner as a debt collector is liable under section 813 for failure to comply with a provision of this title.

**§ 813. Civil liability [15 USC 1692k]**

(a) Except as otherwise provided by this section, any debt collector who fails to comply with any provision of this title with respect to any person is liable to such person in an amount equal to the sum of --

(1) any actual damage sustained by such person as a result of such failure;

(2) (A) in the case of any action by an individual, such additional damages as the court may allow, but not exceeding $1,000; or

(B) in the case of a class action, (i) such amount for each named plaintiff as could be recovered under subparagraph (A), and (ii) such amount as the court may allow for all other class members, without regard to a minimum individual recovery, not to exceed the lesser of $500,000 or 1 per centum of the net worth of the debt collector; and

(3) in the case of any successful action to enforce the foregoing liability, the costs of the action, together with a reasonable attorney's fee as determined by the court. On a finding by the court that an action under this section was brought in bad faith and for the purpose of harassment, the court may award to the defendant attorney's fees reasonable in relation to the work expended and costs.

(b) In determining the amount of liability in any action under subsection (a), the court shall consider, among other relevant factors --

(1) in any individual action under subsection (a)(2)(A), the frequency and persistence of noncompliance by the debt collector, the nature of such noncompliance, and the extent to which such noncompliance was intentional; or

(2) in any class action under subsection (a)(2)(B), the frequency and persistence of noncompliance by the debt collector, the nature of such noncompliance, the resources of the debt collector, the number of persons adversely affected, and the extent to which the debt collector's noncompliance was intentional.

(c) A debt collector may not be held liable in any action brought under this title if the debt collector shows by a preponderance of evidence that the violation was not intentional and resulted from a bona fide error notwithstanding the maintenance of procedures reasonably adapted to avoid any such error.

(d) An action to enforce any liability created by this title may be brought in any appropriate United States district court without regard to the amount in controversy, or in any other court of competent jurisdiction, within one year from the date on which the violation occurs.

(e) No provision of this section imposing any liability shall apply to any act done or omitted in good faith in conformity with any advisory opinion of the Commission, notwithstanding that after such act or omission has occurred, such opinion is amended, rescinded, or determined by judicial or other authority to be invalid for any reason.

**§ 814. Administrative enforcement [15 USC 1692l]**

(a) Compliance with this title shall be enforced by the Commission, except to the extent that enforcement of the requirements imposed under this title is specifically committed to another agency under subsection (b). For purpose of the exercise by the Commission of its functions and powers under the Federal Trade Commission Act, a violation of this title shall be deemed an unfair or deceptive act or practice in violation of that Act. All of the functions and powers of the Commission under the Federal Trade Commission Act are available to the Commission to enforce compliance by any person with this title, irrespective of whether that person is engaged in commerce or meets any other jurisdictional tests in the Federal Trade Commission Act, including the power to enforce the provisions of this title in the same manner as if the violation had been a violation of a Federal Trade Commission trade regulation rule.

(b) Compliance with any requirements imposed under this title shall be enforced under --

(1) section 8 of the Federal Deposit Insurance Act, in the case of --

(A) national banks, by the Comptroller of the Currency;

(B) member banks of the Federal Reserve System (other than national banks), by the Federal Reserve Board; and

(C) banks the deposits or accounts of which are insured by the Federal Deposit Insurance Corporation (other than members of the Federal Reserve System), by the Board of Directors of the Federal Deposit Insurance Corporation;

(2) section 5(d) of the Home Owners Loan Act of 1933, section 407 of the National Housing Act, and sections 6(i) and 17 of the Federal Home Loan Bank Act, by the Federal Home Loan Bank Board (acting directing or through the Federal Savings and Loan Insurance Corporation), in the case of any institution subject to any of those provisions;

(3) the Federal Credit Union Act, by the Administrator of the National Credit Union Administration with respect to any Federal credit union;

(4) subtitle IV of Title 49, by the Interstate Commerce Commission with respect to any common carrier subject to such subtitle;

(5) the Federal Aviation Act of 1958, by the Secretary of Transportation with respect to any air carrier or any foreign air carrier subject to that Act; and

(6) the Packers and Stockyards Act, 1921 (except as provided in section 406 of that Act), by the Secretary of Agriculture with respect to any activities subject to that Act.

(c) For the purpose of the exercise by any agency referred to in subsection (b) of its powers under any Act referred to in that subsection, a violation of any requirement imposed under this title shall be deemed to be a violation of a requirement imposed under that Act. In addition to its powers under any provision of law specifically referred to in subsection (b), each of the agencies referred to in that subsection may exercise, for the purpose of enforcing compliance with any requirement imposed under this title any other authority conferred on it by law, except as provided in subsection (d).

(d) Neither the Commission nor any other agency referred to in subsection (b) may promulgate trade regulation rules or other regulations with respect to the collection of debts by debt collectors as defined in this title.

**§ 815. Reports to Congress by the Commission [15 USC 1692m]**

(a) Not later than one year after the effective date of this title and at one-year intervals thereafter, the Commission shall make reports to the Congress concerning the administration of its functions under this title, including such recommendations as the Commission deems necessary or appropriate. In addition, each report of the Commission shall include its assessment of the extent to which compliance with this title is being achieved and a summary of the enforcement actions taken by the Commission under section 814 of this title.

(b) In the exercise of its functions under this title, the Commission may obtain upon request the views of any other Federal agency which exercises enforcement functions under section 814 of this title.

**§ 816. Relation to State laws [15 USC 1692n]**

This title does not annul, alter, or affect, or exempt any person subject to the provisions of this title from complying with the laws of any State with respect to debt collection practices, except to the extent that those laws are inconsistent with any provision of this title, and then only to the extent of the inconsistency. For purposes of this section, a State law is not inconsistent with this title if the protection such law affords any consumer is greater than the protection provided by this title.

**§ 817. Exemption for State regulation [15 USC 1692o]**

The Commission shall by regulation exempt from the requirements of this title any class of debt collection practices within any State if the Commission determines that under the law of that State that class of debt collection practices is subject to requirements substantially similar to those imposed by this title, and that there is adequate provision for enforcement.

**§ 818. Effective date [15 USC 1692 note]**

This title takes effect upon the expiration of six months after the date of its enactment, but section 809 shall apply only with respect to debts for which the initial attempt to collect occurs after such effective date.

Approved September 20, 1977

**ENDNOTES**

1. So in original; however, should read "604(a)(3)."

**LEGISLATIVE HISTORY:**

Public Law 95-109 [H.R. 5294]

HOUSE REPORT No. 95-131 (Comm. on Banking, Finance, and Urban Affairs).

SENATE REPORT No. 95-382 (Comm. on Banking, Housing, and Urban Affairs).

CONGRESSIONAL RECORD, Vol. 123 (1977):

Apr. 4, considered and passed House.

Aug. 5, considered and passed Senate, amended.

Sept. 8, House agreed to Senate amendment.

WEEKLY COMPILATION OF PRESIDENTIAL DOCUMENTS, Vol. 13, No. 39:

Sept. 20, Presidential statement.

**AMENDMENTS:**

SECTION 621, SUBSECTIONS (b)(3), (b)(4) and (b)(5) were amended to transfer certain administrative enforcement responsibilities, pursuant to Pub. L. 95-473, § 3(b), Oct. 17, 1978. 92 Stat. 166; Pub. L. 95-630, Title V. § 501, November 10, 1978, 92 Stat. 3680; Pub. L. 98-443, § 9(h), Oct. 4, 1984, 98 Stat. 708.

SECTION 803, SUBSECTION (6), defining "debt collector," was amended to repeal the attorney at law exemption at former Section (6)(F) and to redesignate Section 803(6)(G) pursuant to Pub. L. 99-361, July 9, 1986, 100 Stat. 768. For legislative history, see H.R. 237, HOUSE REPORT No. 99-405 (Comm. on Banking, Finance and Urban Affairs). CONGRESSIONAL RECORD: Vol. 131 (1985): Dec. 2, considered and passed House. Vol. 132 (1986): June 26, considered and passed Senate.

SECTION 807, SUBSECTION (11), was amended to affect when debt collectors must state (a) that they are attempting to collect a debt and (b) that information obtained will be used for that purpose, pursuant to Pub. L. 104-208 § 2305, 110 Stat. 3009 (Sept. 30, 1996).

# The War Chest
# Appendix B – The FDCPA

<u>First Response Letter</u> (after collection letter received)

The first response letter following this page is a letter which is designed to place the creditor on notice that you are requesting specific information concerning the debt. This letter invokes your rights under the Fair Debt Collection Practices Act (FDCPA), but without specifically mentioning the law. The letter contains the following critical requests and notices:

Demand for verification of the debt – stops all collection efforts including lawsuits until verification is provided.
The letter explains that calls are inconvenient unless they are made at a specific phone number during specific hours.
The letter demands that the collector not call the place of employment.
The letter demands that the collector not call the debtor's cell phone.

The letter purposely does little more other than to invoke basic protections under the FDCPA. In the event that the collector already committed violations of the FDCPA, and you have collected evidence (phone recordings, other previous letters, witnesses or third parties who answered the phone or overheard your conversation), then you are ready to send a more powerful letter designed to defeat the debt collector in its efforts to collect. As mentioned in the book, you do not want to threaten a FDCPA violation until you have some evidence. Otherwise, the collector will be very careful, and if the collector knows it has not committed any violations, the matter may be sent directly to an attorney with a request file a lawsuit.

Sample Letter – Initial to Debt Collector
(Include only those provisions as applicable)

---

Don Debtor
123 High Street
Anywhere, AZ 85310

December 4, 2024

GFL Financial
3420 Springdale Blvd.
Boston MA 02135

*via certified mail return receipt requested, receipt no. 457319-67234-13 and regular US Mail*

Re: Your Account No. 12-1233659

Dear GFL Financial:

I have received your letter dated March 15, 2013, wherein you advised that you are serving as a debt collector to collect an account for Bank of America, as referenced above.

At this time, I am requesting that you provide verification of the debt, including the following specific information: Please provide the name and address and phone number of the entity you represent. Also, please advise whether or not this is the original creditor. If not, please provide the name, address and phone number of the original creditor. Please furnish information regarding the card member agreement, and any other documents which relate to this debt. Also, please provide information that sufficiently explains how all interest, late fees, and attorney fees were charged. Please provide me any documents that evidence my agreement to any terms of the account, including the original application, and purchase/charge receipts. Please provide proof of your ownership of the debt. If you do not own the debt, and you are acting as a debt collector for another entity, please provide verification that the other entity actually owns or otherwise has the right to collect on this debt.

Letter to GFL Financial
December 4, 2024
Page 2

Recently, you, or someone on your behalf, phoned to discuss this debt. Please do not call any number other than (555) 369-4125, which is my home phone, where I may be reached during the hours of 5:30 PM until 8:00 PM Pacific Standard Time. Phone calls at any other hours or at any other phone numbers are inconvenient to me. Also, please be advised that my employer does not permit me to receive any phone calls at work. Also, do not call my cell phone, as my cell phone is not allowed to ring while I am at work, and I must reserve the limited call allowance for family emergencies and essential communications.

I noticed that in your letter you did not provide a fax number available for me to send correspondence. Please provide a fax number in order that I may be able to promptly communicate to your office in writing, as may be necessary.

Sincerely,

Don Jones

Sample Letter – FDCPA **Violation** Letter to Debt Collector
(Include only those provisions as applicable)

---

Don Debtor
123 High Street
Anywhere, AZ 85310

December 5, 2024

GFL Financial
3420 Springdale Blvd.
Boston MA 02135

*via certified mail return receipt requested, receipt no. 457319-67234-13 and regular US Mail*

Re: Your Account No. 12-1233659

Dear GFL Financial:

I have received your letters dated March 15, April 1 and April 10, 2013. Additionally, you have called my home on five separate occasions. Such phone calls were harassing and intimidating, and were made at times that I had already notified you were inconvenient to me.

Additional clauses as necessary:

[Your company called me at work, even though I notified you that my employer does not allow such phone calls]

[Your company identified itself as a debt collector to people other than me, including the following: my sister, my roommate, my coworker.]

[Your company threatened to put me in jail if I do not pay the debt.]

I have evidence of each of the above violations.

The foregoing conduct on the part of your company constitutes violations of the Fair Debt Collection Practices Act [FDCPA]. Also, I am aware that such conduct violates requirements and regulations governing debt collectors under (State) law.

I am again informing you that I dispute the validity of this debt. I have demanded verification of the debt, but you have not provided anything more than a printout summary of what is in your computer system. I demand complete validation of the entire debt as set forth in my previous letter.

Letter to GFL Financial
April 15, 2013
Page 2

I am demanding that you stop all collection activity against me. I'm demanding that you do not report adverse credit information to credit bureaus as this is a disputed debt. In the event a report is made to the credit bureau that is false and misleading, you are advised that I intend to take action pursuant to my rights under the Fair Credit Reporting Act [FCRA]. Additionally, I am advising of my intent to take action under State laws available to me.

I am demanding that you close this matter. I will be seeing an attorney if I do not receive an immediate appropriate response on the part of your company. I have been advised to seek out a class-action law firm, as apparently there is a pattern and practice in your company of abusing debtors through improper collection procedures. Also, there may be some question about whether or not the financing documents comply with the federal Truth in Lending Act (TILA).

*[If you know you owe a legitimate debt, and you have no defense, and you have evidence that the collector has committed FDCPA violations, you may wish to include a statement such as:* "At this time, I am willing to enter into a mutual release of claims in order to close this matter. In the event that your company desires to fully resolve and settle my FDCPA claims, I am agreeable to a mutual release whereby neither the debtor nor the collector have any obligations. I am unwilling to release my claims against your company without a full and complete release regarding the alleged debt which is in dispute. Please let me know promptly if a mutual release is desired."]

I will await your prompt reply.

Sincerely,

Don Jones

cc: John Jones, Attorney at Law
Jones Law Firm

*(If your attorney permits, place his name as a "cc" showing "copy mailed")*

## Final Demand to Collection Attorney

This final letter to the collection attorney speaks loudly in terms of the intent on the part of the debtor to bring a counterclaim and assert rights under federal and state law, in the event that a lawsuit is filed against the debtor. Again, this letter is only a sample, and some of the provisions in the letter may not specifically apply.

In responding to a debt collection effort, you are not required to identify each and every perceived violation in a letter. Quite often, the attorney will request that you explain the violations. While you have the right and opportunity to do so, there is no legal requirement that you engage in a letter war with the collection attorney. However, if you do have sufficient evidence of the violation, communicating this information in advance of litigation could cause the debt case to never materialize.

The purpose of a letter of this kind is to make clear to the attorney that not only will you bring valid claims against the creditor or debt collector, but that you also will undertake to present claims, to the extent they are supported by evidence, against the lawyer and his firm.

The purpose of this sample letter is not to encourage you to threaten the collection lawyer when the collection lawyer has not committed any violation. However, if you have already disputed the debt in writing, and the lawyer sends you a letter thereafter, he is on notice as to letters you have already sent to the collector. Accordingly, his attempt to collect now amounts to an FDCPA violation. Also, if his staff made calls to you to seek collection, violations may have occurred.

Be sure and modify the letter as necessary for your particular situation.

Letter to Collection Attorney
(Include only those provisions as applicable)

---

Don Debtor
123 High Street
Anywhere, AZ 85310

December 5, 2024

Max Cheatum
Attorney at Law
Doowie, Cheatum & Howe, P.C.
123 Crook Tower Ave. Ste. 2100
Phoenix AZ 85001

*via certified mail return receipt requested, receipt no. 457319-67234-13 and regular US Mail*

Re: Your Client, GFL Financial, Account No. 12-1233659

Dear Mr. Cheatum:

I have received your letter dated October 31, 2024, wherein you advised that you are serving as attorney in effort to collect an account for GFL Financial, as referenced above.

Through previous letters, I have requested validation of the debt. Copies of such letters are enclosed. Please be advised that I have proof of service of these letters. Also, I have communicated that the debt is disputed.

Previously, I notified your office of specific violations of law on the part of your client. I am likewise advising your law firm of my intent to file a claim for specific violations against your law firm for ongoing violations of the Fair Debt Collection Practices Act (FDCPA). Please be advised that in the event suit is filed upon the alleged debt that I intend to present counterclaims and/or separate legal proceedings with respect to FDCPA violations.

As I previously informed, I am concerned that Truth in Lending Act (TILA) violations occurred with respect to the transaction at issue. In light of the fact that the debt is disputed and that there is no apparent validity in your pursuit of such claim, to continue to collect on an invalid debt amounts to additional separate violations of the FDCPA.

I understand that I have right to request that the appropriate court certify my case as a class action case, to be advanced on behalf of all consumers who have been victims of the same violations of law. I am aware of industry practices on the part of debt collectors and their collection attorneys to seek default judgments upon claims that lack validity. Statistically, it has been shown that one out of three collection cases are not legally valid claims, but that such cases result in default judgments in over 90% of case filings. In the event a case is filed, I will not be defaulting, by not filing an appropriate answer. In the event of a counterclaim, I will ask my attorneys to exercise my right of discovery, as to my case as well as to other class members if the case is certified as a class action. It will be my intent in representing class members to fully explore the collector and its law firm's practices of seeking default judgments, in cases which lack merit.

At this time, I am willing to resolve all claims through your office advising that the disputed debt is canceled in full, and that appropriate reporting occur to credit bureaus that the balance of the account is zero. In such situation, I am agreeable to a full and complete release as to any and all claims against your clients, and your firm.

Please do not interpret my letter as a threat. I simply am asserting my rights under state and federal law, and assuring that you are on notice that I will be moving forward with valid claims that are supported by evidence, in the event that suit is filed.

Please allow me to reiterate that I dispute the validity of this debt and that I request verification/validation as required by law.

I am requesting the name, address and telephone number of the original creditor. I am requesting proof that your client has legal ownership of the debt.

I am requesting full explanation and documentation concerning calculation of all interest charges, late fees, and other costs. I am requesting a copy of the original financing transaction documents, including all changes or supplements to any terms or conditions. I am requesting the original documentation that explained finance charges, as required under the Truth in Lending Act (TILA) and state law. I am requesting to see all documents that I signed, or for which there exists an e-signature. I am requesting documentation as to all protocol and procedures related to e-signing documents.

I am requesting that you refrain from further collection procedures until all of the foregoing disclosures have been provided, pursuant to my rights under the FDCPA. I am requesting that the account not be reported to credit reporting agencies, as the account is disputed.

I will await your reply to the foregoing matters.

Sincerely,

Don Jones

cc: (My Attorney)

**DON DEBTOR**
123 High Street
Anywhere, AZ 85301
Defendant
(555) 321-3210

**IN THE SUPERIOR COURT OF THE STATE OF ARIZONA**

**IN AND FOR THE COUNTY OF MARICOPA**

| | |
|---|---|
| **GFL FINANCIAL,** | **Case No.: CV2013-021394** |
| **Plaintiff,** | |
| **vs.** | |
| **DON DEBTOR,** | **ANSWER TO COMPLAINT** |
| **Defendant.** | |

NOW COMES, DON DEBTOR, (hereafter referred to as "Defendant") and hereby files his original Answer to the Complaint, admitting and denying the enumerated assertions and paragraphs set forth in Plaintiffs' Complaint, as follows:

Defendant admits the allegations of Paragraphs 1, 2, 3, 9, 13 and 21 of the Complaint.

Defendant denies the allegations set forth at Paragraphs 3, 5, 6, 7, 8, 9, 10, 12, 15, 16, 17, 18, 19, 20, 22, 23, and 24 of the Complaint.

Defendant is without sufficient information to admit or deny the allegations of Paragraphs 4, 11 and 14 of the Complaint; and accordingly, such paragraphs are denied.

Defendant denies the prayer for relief, and all subparts.

Except as expressly admitted, all of the remaining allegations and averments set forth within Plaintiff's Complaint are denied.

AFFIRMATIVE DEFENSES

Defendant asserts the following affirmative defenses, each of which defeats Plaintiff's claims and causes of action:

Defendant asserts that Defendant is not liable in the capacity in which defendant has been sued.

*[The above paragraph is used when the named individual defendant does not owe the debt. For example, if the debt is a debt of the individual's closely held corporation, or if the debt was incurred on the half of an employer or another person.]*

Defendant asserts that the case should be dismissed for failure of the Plaintiff to have joined an indispensable party.

*[The above paragraph would be used in certain jurisdictions to again point out that the defendant is not liable for the debt, that someone else is liable, urging that such other person must be joined to the lawsuit, or the lawsuit should be dismissed.]*

Defendant asserts that he is not liable as the underlying obligation was discharged in bankruptcy.

*[This paragraph would only be used if there was a previous bankruptcy case that discharged the debt.]*

Defendant alleges a failure of consideration.

*[This affirmative defense would be used where the debtor did not receive what was expected as part of the transaction.]*

Defendant alleges that Plaintiff's claims are barred by the applicable statute of limitations.

*[This paragraph should always be included if the debt is too old to be collected. Statute limitations are generally measured from the date of default. Remember, most States have statutes of limitations that are much shorter for open account debts (credit cards), as opposed to ordinary written contracts.]*

Defendant urges that the Complaint should be dismissed, for the reason that such Complaint fails to state a claim upon which relief may be granted.

*[The above paragraph would be utilized if the Plaintiff's Complaint is not clear as to the basis for which liability is alleged.]*

Defendant asserts that Plaintiff lacks standing as to claims being asserted.

*[This Affirmative Defense is asserted to require that the Creditor establish ownership of the debt.]*

To the extent that the Plaintiff may recover upon its claims, Defendant asserts that such claims must be offset against Defendant's Counterclaims against Plaintiff, which include the following:

Plaintiff has committed violations of the Fair Debt Collections Practices Act (FDCPA) as set forth in Defendant's Counterclaim filed with the Court.

Plaintiff has violated provisions of the Truth in Lending Act (TILA), which entitles Plaintiff to recover actual and statutory damages, including double finance charges assessed.

Plaintiff has committed violations of state law in its collection procedures *[this allegation must confirm with State laws in the State where the consumer is sued or the State in which the consumer was located at the time of entering into the transaction.]*

Plaintiff has failed to mitigate its damages.

*[This paragraph to be used where the Creditor failed to apply lawful credits (i.e. failed to utilize credit life or disability insurance, failed to sell collateral and apply funds to the debt.]*

Plaintiff has failed to satisfy all conditions precedent to recovery. Specifically, Plaintiff was contractually obligated to seek payment of the obligation from *(credit disability insurance, credit life insurance, etc.)*

<u>If a Secured Loan (auto, boat, etc.):</u>

*(if collateral not repossessed or foreclosed)* Defendant asserts a failure on the part of the Plaintiff to mitigate damages. In this respect, Plaintiff has refused and/or neglected to recover the subject collateral. Plaintiff has a responsibility to recover and sell the subject collateral pursuant to the Security Agreement to offset the debt and to mitigate damages.

*(If collateral repossessed and sold)* Defendant asserts a failure on the part of the Plaintiffs to mitigate damages. In this respect, it is alleged that the Plaintiff failed to sell the subject collateral in a commercially reasonable manner.

*[This paragraph to be used where the Creditor failed to sell the collateral in a commercially reasonable manner in order to get a fair price,*

*thereafter, crediting the debt by the sum recovered.]*

13. Filing and service of this suit violates the Fair Debt Collections Practices Act. (FDCPA). Defendant has demanded validation of the debt, which has not been provided. *(If applicable.)*

14. Interest rates, charges and penalties applied to the transactions forming the basis of litigation are usurious and excessive, rendering the contract unconscionable and unenforceable." *(usury defense – typically state law)*

*15.* The Account has been resolved through settlement with the creditor. The claim is improper given full accord and satisfaction. (if applicable). (*This is referred to as the accord and satisfaction defense.)*

REQUEST FOR RELIEF

To the extent that Defendant may hereafter be required to secure the services of a licensed attorney to defend the present action. Defendant should be awarded his reasonable and necessary attorney fees and costs of litigation, as allowed by law.

WHEREFORE, premises considered, Defendant prays that the Court dismiss Plaintiff's claims, and that the Court afford Defendant relief at law and equity, to which Defendant is justly entitled.

DATED this 15th day of January 2025,

**DON DEBTOR**
123 High Street
Anywhere, AZ 85301
Defendant
(555) 321-3210

By /s/Don Debtor
Don Debtor

**DEFENDANT**

ORIGINAL of the foregoing, filed
this 15th day of January 2025
with the Superior Court, Maricopa County:

COPY of the foregoing delivered via United States Mail to:

Max Cheatum
Attorney at Law
Doowie, Cheatum & Howe, P.C.
123 Crook Tower Ave. Ste. 2100
Phoenix AZ 85001

*/s/Don Debtor*
Don Debtor

**DON DEBTOR**
123 High Street
Anywhere, AZ 85301
Defendant
(555) 321-3210

**IN THE SUPERIOR COURT OF THE STATE OF ARIZONA**

**IN AND FOR THE COUNTY OF MARICOPA**

| | |
|---|---|
| **GFL FINANCIAL,**<br><br>**Plaintiff,**<br>**vs.**<br><br>**DON DEBTOR,**<br><br>**Defendant.** | **Case No.: CV2013-021394**<br><br><br><br>**COUNTERCLAIM** |

NOW COMES, DON DEBTOR, (hereafter referred to as "Defendant" and/or "Counter-Plaintiff") and hereby files his COUNTERCLAIM against Plaintiff, GFL Financial (hereafter referred to as "Plaintiff" and/or "Counter-Defendant"), alleging by way of cause of action the following:

1. Plaintiff/Counter-Defendant, GFL Financial, is a [*state*] corporation engaged in the business of collecting debt in this state with its principal place of business located at [*address*]. The principal purpose of Counter-Defendant is the collection of debts in this state and defendant regularly attempts to collect debts alleged to be due another.

2. *(if joining other collectors or the collection attorney)* Third-Party Defendant [*name*], also known as ____________, is a natural person employed by Defendant [*name*] as a collector at all times relevant to this Counterclaim. Such person/law firm also engaged in collection practices in effort to collect the debt that is the subject of this litigation. Such *person/entity* is hereby joined to the action as an additional defendant with respect to Counter-Plaintiff's counterclaims.

3. Counter-Defendant *(and Third Party Defendant)* is/are engaged in

the collection of debts from consumers using the mail and telephone. Counter-Defendant regularly attempts to collect consumer debts alleged to be due to another. Defendant is a "debt collector" as defined by the FDCPA, 15 U.S.C. § 1692a(6).

## ***FACTUAL ALLEGATIONS***
## ***FCDPA VIOLATIONS***

4. By correspondence on the letterhead of [*name*], dated ____________, Counter-Defendant mailed a collection letter under the name of GFL Financial to Counter-Plaintiff, demanding payment of a debt in the amount of ____________ allegedly due to [*creditor*]. A copy is attached hereto as Exhibit A. *(Attach letters that violate FDCPA).*

5. Exhibit A was received by Mr. or Ms. [*name*] at his/her residence in [*city, state*].

6. The alleged debt of Mr. or Ms. [*name*] claimed in Exhibit A was incurred for personal, family, or household services, i.e. (*retail charges of food, clothing and necessaries, payday loan, auto loan, etc.)*

7. Exhibit A stated:

[*Quote the offensive language.*]

Such statements, as presented, violate the FDCPA.

8. In addition to the foregoing, Counter-Defendant was guilty of the following acts and/or omissions constituting separate violations of the Fair Debt Collection Practices Act (FDCPA), 15 U.S.C. Section 1692 et seq.:

a) Counter-Defendant made phone calls at inconvenient times and hours.

b) Counter-Defendant attempted to collect the debt by phone at Counter-Plaintiff's place of work, after being notified that the employer did not permit such phone calls.

c) Counter-Defendant communicated it was attempting to collect a debt to third parties other than Counter-Plaintiff. Such third parties include Counter-Plaintiff's mother, roommate and coworker.

d) Counter-Defendant communicated with Counter-Plaintiff, without providing proper information that it was "attempting to collect a debt and that any information would be used for such purpose."

e) Counter-Defendant continued to engage in collection efforts after being informed in writing to cease and desist, or otherwise after having been informed in writing that Counter-Plaintiff disputed the debt as not owed.

f) Upon being notified that Counter-Plaintiff disputed the debt and demanded validation, the creditor continued collection efforts without providing appropriate validation.

g) Counter-Defendant made improper and unlawful threats towards Counter-Plaintiff.

h) Counter-Defendant's authorized representative communicated by phone that she was affiliated with a "law firm," and that she was calling from the "legal department."

i) Counter-Defendant improperly suggested that Counter-Plaintiff would have his student loans recalled.

j) Counter-Defendant was abusive in its tone and language, using terms such as "you should get a better job," and referring to Counter-Plaintiff as a "deadbeat."

k) Counter-Defendant left inappropriate messages within voicemail which was accessible and actually heard by third parties other than the Counter-Plaintiff.

***(Add as many subparagraphs as appropriate and which refer to specific violations.)***

## *TILA VIOLATIONS*

9. In addition to the foregoing, Counter-Defendant was guilty of the following acts and/or omissions constituting separate violations of the Truth in

Lending Act (TILA) (Regulation Z, fifteen U.S.C. section 1601 et seq.), and parallel provisions of state law:

a) Counter-Defendant failed to provide proper disclosure as to the manner in calculation of finance charges, as required under the TILA.

b) Counter-Defendant assessed additional costs and fees as part of the finance charges that were not supported by the original contract, amounting to a violation of TILA.

c) Upon information and belief, Counter-Defendant engaged in the practice of leading the consumer to believe that lower interest and finance charges would be applied to the debt, yet thereafter assessed higher finance charges.

d.) Counter-Defendant did not provide all legal disclosures as required by law, entitling Counter-Plaintiff to damages and rescission, as warranted.

10. As a result of the acts alleged above, Counter-Plaintiff suffered severe humiliation and embarrassment, depression, and anxiety. Counter-Plaintiff's emotional distress has been so severe as to cause lost time at work, use of sick leave, weight loss, expenses for medication and additional day care for dependents. Counter-Plaintiff has also sustained additional financial loss and damages due to improper interest charges and assessment of fees and charges.

## *CLAIM FOR RELIEF*

11. Counter-Defendants violated the FDCPA and TILA, such that Counter-Defendant is liable to Counter-Plaintiff for declaratory judgment that defendants' conduct violated the FDCPA and TILA, for all actual damages, statutory damages, and costs and attorney fees.

12. Counter-Plaintiff reserves the right to seek class certification of this Counterclaim, to permit the case to proceed on behalf of all consumers who are like situated. A Motion for Class Certification is not being presented at this

time, although Counter-Defendant, *Third-Party Defendant*, and the Court are hereby alerted that class certification may be sought.

WHEREFORE, Counter-Plaintiff respectfully requests that judgment be entered against Counter-Defendant (*and Third Party Defendant)* for the following:

Declaratory judgment that Counter-Defendant's (*and Third Party Defendant's)* conduct violated the FDCPA;
Declaratory judgment that Counter-Defendant's (*and Third Party Defendant's)* conduct violated the TILA.
Declaratory judgment that Counter-Defendant's (*and Third Party Defendant's)* conduct violated provisions of state law.
Actual damages;
Statutory damages pursuant to federal law;
Punitive Damages;
Costs and reasonable attorney fees.
For such other and further relief as the Court may deem just and proper.

DATED this 15th day of January 2025,

**DON DEBTOR**
123 High Street
Anywhere, AZ 85301
Defendant
(555) 321-3210

By /s/Don Debtor
Don Debtor

**DEFENDANT/COUNTER-PLAINTIFF**

***DEMAND FOR JURY TRIAL***

Please take notice that Defendant/Counter-Plaintiff [*name*] demands trial by jury in this action.

________________________
Counter-Plaintiff

ORIGINAL of the foregoing, filed
this 15TH day of January, 2025
with the Superior Court, Maricopa County:

COPY of the foregoing delivered via United States Mail to:

Max Cheatum
Attorney at Law
Doowie, Cheatum & Howe, P.C.
123 Crook Tower Ave. Ste. 2100
Phoenix AZ 85001

*/s/Don Debtor*
Don Debtor

Made in the USA
Monee, IL
19 October 2026

66036198R00148